DAVID LEE

*The Evolution
and Revolution of
Golf Instruction*

Printed in U.S.A.

ISBN 0-9645478-7-2

Acknowledgments

My most sincere thanks to Jack Nicklaus for his endorsement in 1977 of the original concepts of the Gravity system which inspired the research of the last seventeen years.

To Adam Anthony, my partner in Gravity Sports Concepts, Inc., whose steadfast belief in the techniques means more to me than I can convey.

To Dr. Gregory Mihailoff and Mr. George Butterworth for their contributions to the manuscript and their belief in the rightness of the information.

To Chi Chi Rodriguez, Rocky Thompson, all of the golf professionals and my other students who have been willing to open their minds and approach this game from a different point of view.

To Karen Anderson for the cover art and diagrams.

And most of all to my wife Crickett, and my children Autumn and Danny, who have supported and tolerated me through much of the research and the writing of this book.

Thank You All!

Contents

About the Author and His Methods

Foreword by George Butterworth

Introduction by David Lee

About the Author and His Methods

The **"GRAVITY"** teaching system is a revolutionary method of teaching golf which has been under development and refinement for the last eighteen years. The author, David Lee, has been a PGA professional since 1965.

Lee, a native of Hot Springs, Arkansas, played the PGA tour from 1970-72. Having trained himself since childhood as an upper body player in the style of Arnold Palmer, he quickly realized that as a tour player he did not have the strength to swing consistently in that manner. "For hours I used to sit on the practice tee and watch Jack Nicklaus, Lee Trevino and Tom Weiskopf hit golf balls. It certainly didn't take a rocket scientist to figure out that they hit the ball better than most of the other players. Their shots were definitely straighter than mine, obviously made with less effort, and I sensed a different timing altogether in their swing mechanics."

Unable to find anyone willing or capable of teaching him the "feel" of this unique swing, and finding nothing available to read on how to change power sources, Lee set about trying to make the swing change on his own. "I spent three months trying to hit one solid shot that didn't hook to some degree." One day, totally by accident, while making some swings with his left leg in full motion (see page 128), he literally "stumbled" across the 2:1 timing that allows the lower body to power the golf swing. "Most people swing in a 1:1 timing, where the club goes back as the weight moves to the right foot, and comes through as the weight moves to the left foot. In Jack Nicklaus' swing the body weight moves fully to the right and back to the left during the takeaway. The upper body, in the backswing, moves at an average of one half the speed of the weight transfer. It's like playing the drums, with one hand playing one beat, and the other hand playing a different beat, or like patting your head and rubbing your stomach at the same time. It's not something you can think your way through, you just have to do it."

Once Lee had effectively made the change in power source, his attitude toward the game changed completely. "After you learn to power the swing by lower body **rotation and reactionary movement** instead of **applied upper body force**, the swing becomes not only easy to repeat, but also effortless. I can't believe I fought it for so many years!"

With the new swing, Lee was more determined than ever to develop into a great player. However, an injury to his left wrist in the winter of 1976 left him with a severely weakened hand and a doubtful playing career. At that turning point in his life, he decided to focus his attention toward developing a method for teaching the new swing he had learned. Over the last eighteen years he has developed not only an unparalleled understanding of swing mechanics, but more importantly, a unique system of **training drills** through which **perfect timing can be rapidly "force fed" into a student, regardless of whether he or she understands the physics principles involved.**

The GRAVITY teaching system can take a player from a complete beginner to a competitive level professional, in a period as short as twelve to eighteen months. To accomplish such a feat, an individual would need to devote a considerable amount of time to his or her game; but even at that, it is only a fraction of the time normally required to develop a sub-par player.

A golfer who learns to play using the GRAVITY system does not have to rely on strength to make the swing. Lee states that, "in a correct swing, distance is controlled predominately through an individual's height, how the right arm is routed (right handed player), and also by the quality of his or her mechanics. A person who is getting older and losing strength, or a female player who never had strength to begin with, need not be concerned about distance. Anyone over four feet tall can develop an adequate arc to hit the ball over two hundred yards when they couple that arc size with proper timing and tension relationships."

The information contained in this book can and will have a dramatic and lasting effect on the rest of your golf life if you can grasp the concept and **will practice using the drills**. Go over the principles until a picture of how to make a mechanically proper swing crystallizes in your mind. The mysterious pieces of the puzzle will all fall into place **once-and-for-always**. Dedicate some time toward understanding the mechanics and be patient with yourself. It requires some considerable study to fully understand the technical relationships between the body parts in a perfect swing. Once you have learned the GRAVITY swing, and realize how easy it is to repeat, you'll be astounded by how much less effort you need to hit the ball. In fact, it requires almost none. When you understand how to use **all** the available leverage forces against the **ball** (instead of partially turning them against yourself) you can hit the ball a long way — and control it as well. With both distance and control going for you, golf becomes the game it should be and you'll enjoy it for the rest of your life. You will be more excited over your possibilities and capabilities than you've ever dreamed. **Believe it.... it's true!**

The drills are the key to easy development of perfect timing within anyone. In a unique way, **the drills** communicate with the subconscious and motor skills areas of the student's brain, while the instructor can only communicate with the conscious mind. Since the incredible subconscious (cerebellum or lower cortex) can handle so many functions simultaneously, **it becomes possible through the drills to program all the necessary moving parts at <u>one</u> time**. If the conscious mind (cerebral or higher cortex) is in control of the learning process, it is practically impossible to learn to coordinate all the moving body parts at once; yet the cerebellum and other parts of your subconscious can perform the task quite easily. The process is truly fascinating and you'll amaze yourself with what you can accomplish in a very short time.

David Lee has been teaching the GRAVITY system exclusively since 1976. He has taught at Houston C.C., Houston, Tx., at Walden on Lake Conroe, Houston, Tx., at Deerwood C.C., Jacksonville, Fla., at Colonial C.C., Fort Worth, Tx., and at the beautiful Black Diamond Ranch Golf and Country Club, in Lecanto, Florida.

The GRAVITY teaching technique has been featured in articles in both Golf Magazine and Golf Digest, and has been personally endorsed in writing by Jack Nicklaus, Chi Chi Rodriguez, and other top professionals.

Foreword
Gravity Golf — A Paradigm Shift
by George Butterworth
BSc Physics
Nottingham University, England

THE RIGHT ANSWER

Maybe I was a bit odd because I liked mathematics as a kid — but it was for a reason. You see, there was always a "right answer" and one could score full marks on a test (however rare the experience). Conversely, if you got the wrong answer, you were just plain wrong.... zero marks.... not some shade of wrong.

This contrasted with other subjects where I never seemed to understand the rules, like English Literature and Art, where I thought my efforts were, on occasion, brilliant and could never understand why my teachers didn't recognize the fact. You see.... there's no "right answer" in the arts and classics, and if the teacher gets out of bed on the wrong side or doesn't like your hair style, he/she can mark you down and never have to explain. That's why I ended up taking physics; not brave enough to take the mathematics degree — but then physics usually has a "right answer" too!

SPORTS, THE RIGHT ANSWER AND GOLF

You would have thought that with this "black and white" mentality that sports would have driven me crazy. On the contrary — although I was not a super-star at any sport, I managed to get close enough to the "right answer" to be captain of the school soccer team, vice-captain of the cricket team, pole-vault for the athletics team etc.... you see, I am well coordinated — a good dancer as well. In fact, I had never doubted my ability to become competent at ANY sport — it was just a matter of time and effort, until....... GOLF!!

It was deliberate that I reserved golf as a sport for my later years, when my decaying body would inevitably fail to get me around the squash court and my reflexes could no longer cope with the speed of "league" table tennis and badminton (serious sports in the UK!). So at the age of forty I decided that it was time to quickly master the art of hitting the little white ball into the hole, so that I could hob-nob with the corporate executives on the golf course and thereby enhance my future career prospects. Since I had previously played sports with the ball moving almost at the speed of light, hitting a stationary ball with a long stick was not going to be a problem...... **wrong!!**

After two years of sheer obstinacy, I finally had to accept the fact that my natural talent alone and occasional visits to the golf range were not getting me to tour standard. So I decided to go in search of golf's "right answer."

IN SEARCH OF THE "RIGHT ANSWER"

Now, we are not dealing with some abstruse branch of sub-atomic physics, where there is little information available. This is GOLF!.......... access to information on golf is definitely not one of the sport's problems. Furthermore, this is a five hundred year old sport, so there has been ample time to identify, verify and demonstrate the "right answer." Thus, for a trained scientist and an athlete, it should only be a matter of reviewing the literature, observing the experts and a little practice to finally master the sport......**wrong again!!**

It doesn't take a Rhodes scholar to recognize that there are some critical fundamental differences between the swings successfully employed by such golfing legends as Jack Nicklaus, Arnold Palmer, Ben Hogan etc. In fact, there are probably more differences than there are similarities — so how to proceed? Clearly, the scientific approach is to identify those swing factors common among all good players, and then we will have the fundamental elements of the "right answer." Unfortunately, the only question that all golfers give the same answer to is: "what do you feel when you hit that perfect shot?" Answer..... "I feel nothing.... it's absolutely effortless!!" This somehow seemed an inadequate definition for the "right answer" and not something upon which to build my swing.

Some ten years passed during which time I studied every popular book on the game, bought every video I could afford and took golf lessons from a number of golf professionals and every friend who took pity on my suffering. As a result, I was no further to identifying the "right answer" than when I started. In fact, my golf game, my interest and my enjoyment were slowly deteriorating, when, by divine intervention, I relocated to Texas, and met David Lee, the creator of the "right answer"..... GRAVITY golf.... **the holy grail!!**

YES.... BUT WHAT'S THE QUESTION?

At first sight, the golf swing seems to be more like English Literature or Art since you can get "good marks" or win tournaments with radically different swings. But, success and failure are not defined by opinion, style or taste, but in terms of good scientific specification involving such measurable parameters as: swing reliability, distance ball travels per unit energy expended etc.. Provided one clearly defines the specification, there has to be a "right" or at least "<u>best</u> answer."

The specification for the "right swing" is very simple. It is the swing that employs the minimum energy, and which reliably and accurately transports the ball the required distance. Why is "minimum energy" important? **Because the energy used is a direct measure of the efficiency of the swing**. The more upper body and aggressiveness put into the swing, the more energy employed and the lower the efficiency. Conversely, when the swing mechanics are ideal, **no** energy is being wasted on maintaining balance or manipulating the club. The ball just takes off without any apparent effort. That's why the "perfect swing" feels effortless.... **it is!**

WHY **GRAVITY** GOLF?

But what is it about the GRAVITY golf swing that makes it the "right answer?" Two factors uniquely qualify it as the "right swing."

The first is the use of "limp arms," which eliminates the application of destructive and wasteful forces via the arms and shoulders in an effort to "hit" the ball. In teaching the GRAVITY golf swing, David Lee identifies a **"first release"** point after the arms have moved approximately one foot into the backswing. At this point, **all** the tension in the arms and shoulders is removed and the remainder of the swing, through impact, is made with soft arms and the results left to "gravity," centrifugal force and timing! **There is clearly no wasted energy with this approach!**

The second unique aspect of GRAVITY golf is the method of teaching "perfect balance." The use of one-legged drills has been occasionally promoted by others as a bit of a gimmick. However, David Lee employs both one-legged and one-armed drills as **essential foundations** for rapidly teaching GRAVITY golf. Not only do his drills quickly accelerate the rate at which one can become proficient, but the one-legged drills, ultimately teach "perfect balance" — a feeling rarely experienced by the majority of us "hackers" in the golfing community. It doesn't take long for the brain to realize that, when on one leg, the application of unnecessary violence or force in the golf swing can create unacceptable consequences and that the "minimum energy" swing is the answer to survival! In fact, the reducing energy level required to do these drills is a steady measure of progress. As one develops proficiency, the energy level required to swing the club, steadily falls as one approaches the ecstasy of the perfect GRAVITY swing.

GRAVITY GOLF AND THE FIRST LAW
OF MOTION

Simply put, Issac Newton's 1st Law of Motion states that an object will continue to travel in a straight line unless acted upon by an external force. Therefore, if the club is accelerated straight back and then allowed to "free fall," without applying any additional force via the body to change the arc of the swing, the club would automatically return to the starting point through centrifugal force and strike the ball. This principle is fundamental to the GRAVITY golf swing. On this basis, the most reliable and repeatable swing would be the one that minimizes the amount of applied force during the swing which might deflect the club from a perfect arc. The GRAVITY golf swing must qualify as theoretically THE MOST RELIABLE SWING since NO unnecessary external force is applied after the first release.

THE MOST ENERGY EFFICIENT GOLF SWING??

Due to the "soft" arms employed in the perfect GRAVITY golf swing, no energy is wasted in trying to artificially "steer" the golf club or to consciously "hit" the ball. Thus inherently the GRAVITY swing is highly energy efficient.

But there is one other feature of the perfect GRAVITY swing that makes it the most energy efficient.... "perfect balance." But, you say, surely all good swings require perfect balance? Not necessarily.... watch Chi Chi Rodriguez.

Balance problems in the swing primarily result from the speeding arms and club in the down-swing pulling the body forward (toward the toes). The faster the swing, the stronger the centrifugal force that pulls us forward and causes us to occasionally dig the club into the ground behind the ball or "come over the top." In any good golf swing, the body learns to subconsciously "lean" or "fall" backwards to introduce an equal and off-setting force and therefore maintain balance. That's why Chi Chi literally falls away from the ball when he's trying to keep up with the long drivers on the senior tour. He is built so slightly, that he has to fall more than most to off-set the big swing. David Lee refers to this as "counterfall."

When people describe that rare and wonderful swing as being "effortless," they have either accidentally or with great skill, initiated the counterfall correctly and exactly off-set the forward pulling force from the speeding arms and club. It feels terrific! No fight to keep ones balance — the club seems to speed through of its own accord — the ball takes off like a rocket and we end up poised, staring down the fairway, feeling like Jack!

David Lee's use of one-legged drills as a PRIMARY technique for teaching the GRAVITY swing, results in the brain rapidly acquiring a subconscious capability to induce the "correct" counterfall **and thereby produce a perfectly balanced swing**.

JACK AND THE OTHER GOLF "GODS"

A further complication of golf is that we are not all using the same equipment, and I am not referring to the clubs!

16

Some of us suspect that big Jack is not truly mortal. Even if he is.... certainly he has never experienced trying to hit the ball with my body, my coordination and my preconceived notions about the golf swing. The closest he might come is when he has a stiff back and a hangover!

As a consequence, Jack and the other golf greats have no idea what we "humans" feel when we swing the golf club and thus they find it almost impossible to tell us how they do what they do! What's "normal" to them and not worth communicating (even if they could), would be "revolutionary" to you and me. How can someone used to driving a Ferrari most of his life tell me how to get the most out of my 1938 Chevy?

Because of this communication gap, golf is primarily taught through a description of the individual pieces of the swing — the grip, the takeaway, etc..

GRAVITY GOLF — A SYSTEMS APPROACH

One of the problems in science is that, while we might understand how the individual pieces work, complex machines frequently do not perform the way we expect. Unanticipated interactions occur between the various parts and sub-systems with occasional disastrous consequences. **Knowing how the pieces work is not sufficient**.

This same problem plagues the teaching of golf. One only has to browse through the golf magazines to realize that golf instruction is generally focused on how the parts work.

However, as most of us know, adding up the little pieces, in **NO** way guarantees the "right answer" when we attempt to put them into motion.

In teaching GRAVITY golf, David Lee, places as much or more emphasis on the overall "shape and feel" of the swing as he does on basic essential mechanics. In fact, the one-legged drills make the teaching of many of the "parts" **not necessary**. Self preservation is the **most** effective teacher!

I DIDN'T KNOW THAT!

The "first release" is just one of the revolutionary pieces of information that David Lee has discovered about the "right swing." Another "gem" is that over ninety percent of the distance we can drive the ball from a normal stance, can be achieved from one leg! David's understanding of the GRAVITY golf swing is unparalleled and his complete knowledge of the mechanics and forces involved is "music to the ears" to those of us scientists and engineers who play this game.

All this implies that the GRAVITY golf swing is new and has never been discovered. On the contrary — this type of swing has been used by a number of champions over the years, by far the most famous being the "Golden Bear" himself, Jack Nicklaus.... flying right elbow and all!
I know.... you knew the "right answer" already!

GRAVITY GOLF AND [E = MC\2]

Major breakthroughs in science invariably result from someone adopting a radically new way of looking at things — establishing a new frame of reference or paradigm. Einstein did this for physics with his relativity theory and Darwin for evolution with his publication on the origin of the species. In many cases this type of revolutionary thinking was initially misunderstood, ignored and, in some cases, ridiculed by the scientific community.

GRAVITY golf, as taught by David Lee, represents a **major** breakthrough in golf in that **he has identified the "right (answer) swing," introduced a paradigm shift in the depth of understanding of the mechanics of the golf swing, and has developed a radically new method of teaching that accelerates the process and strongly suggests that golf has been taught BACK-TO-FRONT for the last five hundred years!**

Gravity Golf
by David Lee

Introduction

Have you ever wondered why even the most experienced players of this wonderful, but often mystifying game, encounter periods when they lose control of their golf swings? Is it conceivable, that after several hundred years of studying this complex pastime, mankind could have advanced his overall knowledge of swing mechanics no further than, for example, his understanding of the airplane in 1920? If that statement is even remotely true, there is a great deal of sadness attached to it for many folks who have sacrificed a great deal of their lifetime (not to mention a lot of their money, patience, self esteem and dignity) in trying to comprehend and master it. Without question, the game is a constant reminder of the awesome complexity of the human animal. Because of the profound subtleties involved, attempting to coordinate all the physical movements that a consistently repeating golf swing requires, can be (and usually is) a task of mind boggling proportions. Let's not even mention at this time the seemingly countless mental pitfalls with which the game can beguile and torment us.

Wouldn't it be a fantastic experience if all of us at one time or another (and preferably most of the time) could enjoy the exhilaration of being able to hit and control a golf ball like Jack Nicklaus? All nod. Well, if you're one of those awestruck individuals who's concluded that Jack is really an alien superman come down to the earth in golf spikes, then you probably won't get much out of this book. If however, you are bullheaded enough to believe that someday soon you, too, might conquer this game, and that yes.... there really could be a secret to it, read on. You very well might, **and there absolutely is!**

As you are no doubt aware, there are a number of different ways to power a golf swing. Of the four fundamental types of swing, the one which I've labeled the GRAVITY swing (for reasons I will explain) **is the only technique which is in total compliance with the laws of good physics.** For this reason, it is the most reliable from a standpoint of repeatability and withstanding competitive pressure.

In this revolutionary approach to golf instruction and learning, you will be offered profound scientific evidence **that the game has been taught 180 degrees from the most <u>ideal</u> way, since the inception of the sport.** What's more, you'll discover that the great natural forces which Jack and a handful of other players have been fortunate enough to "stumble" across and harness, also exist within your body. Oh!.... excuse me, you knew they were there all the time! Well, trust me.... once you unlock those forces through understanding and some "**correct**" practice, they will serve you faithfully throughout the remainder of your golf life. You'll get the most from your golf swing and maximize your enjoyment of this marvelous game. There is probably not a golfer that ever lived, who didn't long to "give up the struggle." Yet most of us can't seem to quite "let go." Comparatively, it's sort of like learning to juggle. Getting there may appear impossible, but once you've got the knack, it just "ain't that hard." Lean back, open your mind, and learn what Mother Nature can do for your golf game if you will only give her a chance.

By the way, in the preparation of this document I've already been attacked by my golf writer friends for not getting into the "meat" of the material early enough in the book. The first three chapters reflect a lot of my own experience and philosophy, yet they are also preparatory for understanding why one should learn through this technique. The "guts" of this book are in chapters four, five and six. You can skip right to that part if you can't wait to hit it "perfectly" — or you can have a little fun with me getting there. There is no ghost writer involved in the project and anyone with formal writing experience might easily determine that I've never written a book before. If you find a misplaced modifier or a punctuation error, forget about it. This offering is simply me. However, the information pertinent to swing mechanics and how to teach them (which you'll find within these pages) is open to — and welcomes — any constructive opinions. Let's go!

Chapter One

The Bottom Line

WHAT IS A WINNER?

Excuse me Ben, but I believe you're away. Is my ball marker in your line?....... Sorry Jack, I didn't mean to show disrespect by outdriving you again....... Oh!, too bad Arnie, you're in the cactus! Is the pressure of playing with me getting to you?...... rriinnggg!! Dang that alarm clock! Every time I'm about to finish one of those dreams and take my rightful place in history, that stinking thing goes off.

Doesn't every individual, regardless of his or her personal goals, experience fantasies of success? How do we perceive ourselves in the competition of life? When faced with the following questions, to what extent are we willing to sacrifice?

What makes a winner? What does it take to win? Not quite the same, are they? A winner is one who gives completely of himself or herself; trophies or none, regardless of comparisons to other individuals — and is personally satisfied to have done so.

To win at stroke play golf requires shooting the lowest score over a given number of holes. How ridiculously simple, right? Just hit the ball fewer times than anyone else, and fame, fortune and glory are yours for the taking. Only two small problems.... the rules state that it is necessary to count all the strokes and play all the holes. No fair stopping when we get to a number we like. Well Sam, I think 276 will win this thing, let's go in. "But boss.... we've only played 68 holes." How well I know the name of that tune!

WHAT'S IT GONNA' TAKE?

As the game has developed and competition gotten keener, the scope of posting a winning golf score in the 1990's has changed. Natural ability, physical conditioning, technique, discipline to practice, grit ("heart size") and mental self control, are all traits that must be possessed either in part, or in totality, by a winning golfer. In the past it has been possible for a player to win with only one or two of these characteristics. However, to walk off with the trophy nowadays, it is becoming increasingly necessary to be strong in all the categories.

Of the six factors listed, natural ability historically has played a lesser role, simply because golf is generally an acquired skill. Great athletes from other sports have rarely shown an ability to excel at the game without proper training. As time goes on and teaching methods improve, natural athleticism (when coupled with better instructional techniques) will become a more important factor for winning at pro-fessional golf.

Mental self control is a difficult item to rank because its importance increases as the player's technique improves. There is a strong movement today among sports psychologists toward learning to "get out of your own way" and just "let it happen." From my perspective, we might argue all day on whether golf is 95% mental, 50% mental, or 5% mental. It really doesn't matter. What does matter, is that regardless of how perfect your game plan may be, once you "whip it over the fence" a couple of times from the first tee, that perfect plan.... and your perfect attitude, will usually go right down the "port-a-potty" along with the 68 you were going to "let yourself shoot." If the esteemed golf psychologist, Chuck Hogan, thinks that Greg Norman or Seve Ballesteros are going to stand on the eleventh fairway at Augusta, knock it in the lake, and calmly say to themselves, "nice shot," he's wearin' pink underwear! I'm sure that when Raymond Floyd knocked it in that very lake in his 1990 Masters playoff with Nick Faldo, he said those exact words. Splash..... "nice shot, Raymond." Right, and my father is the Pope! You didn't see anyone hustling over to Raymond with a microphone so that we could all hear him say "nice shot" to the world! Raymond pulled that ball because a little tension crept in on him which he failed to deal with, threw his timing off and made him "grab" the change of direction, forcing the swing-plane over the top. It was ever so slight — but enough to ruin Raymond's day. I felt so bad for him that it almost made me sick to my stomach. **My strong conviction is (and will remain) that a consistently repeating swing, and the predictability that accompanies it, must precede a good game plan if there is to be much chance of actually implementing that plan. An exact understanding of how tension affects timing is critical to the ability of dealing with and overcoming its consequences.** In regard to this chicken (repeating technique) or egg (mental self control) question, I feel there is no doubt as to which must come first.... cluck! Until a certain level of shotmaking skill is acquired, it is difficult to even explore the mental side of golf. Confidence will not keep an airplane in the sky, nor will it keep the club in the swing-plane, or the ball on line to the target. Once a dependable technique has been developed and trained into the body, the confidence that accompanies successful shots will then **aid** to control tension and enhance the ability to keep subsequent swings in timing. However, attitude and self control are **not**, and **never will be**, the major determining factors for controlling the golf swing.

For my money, technique ranks first in importance for the modern day golfer, with grit ("heart size") and determination running close behind. Without strong mechanics, however, even an individual with superior "guts," like Arnold Palmer, would have a more difficult time on today's tour than Arnold had in his heyday.

Physical conditioning, and discipline to practice, are of almost equal importance to the modern tournament golfer. There has been a time when grit and discipline to practice (even if the technique was less than desirable) were enough. However, times are changing. In a day where it usually takes at least ten under par or better to win a four day event, there are not many victories for those who let more than a very few shots get away. In fact, there are times, in my opinion, that the demand to execute at such a high level of performance seems to take a lot of the fun from the game. When the fun goes, the primary reason for playing golf.... is lost! End of speech.

O.K., so notwithstanding the fun, maybe you still want to be the next Jack Nicklaus. Perhaps you would just like to see some of your foursome's money begin flowing into your pocket instead of out. What can be done? From my point of view (assuming you possess <u>some</u> of the aforementioned qualities) the developmental procedure for creating a winning golf game would include the following suggestions.

A PLAN

1. **Find yourself an instructor in whom you have faith, who has a genuine interest in seeing you improve.** If one cannot be found, you will find everything you need to know in this book. I also recommend that if you don't have the accompanying video tape, you should get it. Moving pictures help consolidate what usually requires many words and pages to explain. Never feel ashamed to admit that you need help in developing your game. Golf is difficult to learn because of the subtleties and variables involved. I am constantly amazed at the number of people who have been playing for years, still can't break 100, and yet brag about the fact that they never had a lesson in their life. I always laugh, not with them (as my mother taught me), but <u>at</u> them. **THE BEST GOLF DOLLARS YOU WILL EVER SPEND WILL BE THOSE SPENT ON CORRECT INSTRUCTION. THE CONVERSE IS EQUALLY TRUE.** It is extremely important to get started off properly, so that you don't develop habits that later must be corrected in order for you to progress. Remember, **"it is not practice that makes perfect, but perfect practice."** What a true and important statement.... too bad I didn't say it first!

2. **Establish goals for yourself that challenge you to improve; but not so lofty that they prompt you to forget why you took up the game.** For fun.... right? The difference between sanity and senility can be measured in three putt greens — so start off with some realistic goals and re-evaluate them as you improve.

3. **Make time to practice and develop the discipline to stay with your schedule.** Many times you'll get discouraged and feel as though you're regressing, until one day you'll wake up and it will all come together. It does, indeed, take a good deal of correct training to develop a repeating golf swing, so be patient with yourself.

4. **Learn to practice your weaknesses.** Invariably, when I am teaching, the first thing I notice about a new student is that even after being shown what areas of the swing need work, if I turn my back for two minutes, the knucklehead has returned to practicing the things he or she does best. It is only natural to want to do the things which we feel make us look more professional. Being insecure about working on weak areas simply because the shots may be worse for a while, **will only prolong the development.** I can remember a number of occasions during my years on the tour, when a famous player would come to the practice tee and start practicing beside me. Usually he would bring his gallery along with him, and I can remember feeling nervous enough to immediately put away my driver (which is the club I needed to be working on) and pull out my seven iron

which I knew I could hit well every time. Pride goeth before the fall as surely as a bad tee shot goeth over the OB stake. I am proud to say that I never hit a seven iron out of bounds, but then again, who has? My advice.... get on the practice tee, lock your sweaty little fingers around that driver and learn to hit it! It's the most important club in the bag because using it effectively sets up and simplifies your ability to score. So... you wipe out a few tennis players while you're learning.... who cares? Don't be so self conscious. One more time, **practice your weaknesses.**

5. **Condition your body if you wish to play the best golf possible.** Being in shape offers several advantages other than making you look better, feel better and live longer. First, it allows you to fight off fatigue. Fatigue creates tension, which (as you probably are aware) causes **horrible** things to happen in the golf swing. Secondly, it allows margin for error by providing stability in the body — and will help in some circumstances to cover up your swing flaws. In other circumstances, it will help to magnify them. Later in the book, we will discuss in detail how to use strength in a positive way rather than turning it against yourself **(which can easily be done)**. The ability to turn one's strength against oneself is the reason that great athletes don't necessarily make great golfers. However, once **properly** trained, they enjoy considerable advantages over other players. Thirdly, conditioning will allow you to develop greater distance; but again, only if the accompanying strength is properly utilized. Other

noteworthy points are that, on the average, better conditioned individuals think more clearly, as well as being more supple and less injury prone. Spending a few minutes each day rolling around on the floor with Jane Fonda and her good looking athletic pals will improve your golf game (if not your imagination), and in the event that you buy her video tape, it won't hurt Jane either.

6. **You are... what you eat!** Not being a doctor, I don't wish to get into a discussion on diet, but I can assure you from experience, that **if you are desirous of playing the best golf possible, diet is very important. Any athlete will perform best if his body is regularly detoxified and properly fueled with the most nutritious, non-toxic foods**. Horse hockey, right? **Believe it, it's true!**

7. **Know the golf course and learn to develop a good game plan.** Most players throw away many shots needlessly, due in part to the fact that they don't know the course (or their own abilities) well enough to know the most risk-free shots to play. It is very important to know what realistically you can do, as well as what you probably cannot. Learning to know the difference between a solid gamble and a foolish risk.... this means you, Greg Powers (one of my touring pros who likes living on the "edge"), is often the difference between eating steak this week, or throwing your clubs in the trunk of your car and rolling on down

the highway to the nearest "Big Mac." All good professional players know how to play the odds. The better you know your swing, the more consistently it repeats. The better you know the course, the more you can tilt the odds of staying out of trouble in your favor.

8. **Play by the rules and don't cheat!** One of the great characteristics of golf is that it calls upon the individual to face his own shortcomings and deal with bad breaks as part of the game. No one ever teed it up who didn't get his share of unfortunate bounces. The ability to take them in stride and maintain self control plays a large part in becoming a true golfer. Sort of parallels being a decent human being, doesn't it? The old statement made by PGA champion Jerry Barber that "the more I practice, the luckier I get," is and always will be true! If you properly apply yourself, your share of good bounces will come. Play the ball as it lies, the course as you find it, write down **all** your strokes — and you'll come to know golf for the great game it really is. The same golfer could win the U.S. Open, and intentionally break a rule in his club championship, and his reputation for cheating would supersede and outlive that of being a great player. The fact that golf calls upon the integrity of the individual to fairly judge himself and invoke his own penalties, should they be required, sets golf apart as a unique character building experience for those fortunate enough to know and comprehend the sport as it was designed to be. Don't forget either that the rules can often <u>help</u> you instead of penalizing you — <u>if</u> you know them.

9. Learn to visualize what you want to happen. This applies both to winning as well as to individual shots. Let me reiterate that this is easier to do if there is sufficient swing training to realistically expect your shots to come off as planned. Once you develop some predictability in your mechanics, as well as the ability to make the ball do certain things, shot visualization becomes simple. Plan your strategy, picture the shot in your mind, walk to the ball (make sure it's yours) and fire! There is a time to think, and it is definitely not while you are standing over the ball. Grinding your conscious mind when it is time for your subconscious muscle memory to take over, is what sport psychologists call "getting in your own way." It will throw your timing off most every time.

10. **Learn to play quickly!** In a time when golf courses are becoming much more crowded, the game is being made less enjoyable by a lot of individuals who don't know how to play without delay. **Learn to watch where your ball goes, mark the spot in your mind, find it quickly, make a decision, and hit it!** If you want to go for a long walk in the park... by all means do it! If you want to play golf... do that too! But for goodness sake, don't lollygag around. I might be playing behind you and I'm running out of time. Besides, you can rest assured that the less of a mental ordeal you make of the game, the better your scores will be.

11. Above **all, learn to have fun!** My grandmother Pearl (she was one too) used to admonish me; "David, don't take life too seriously.... you won't get out of it alive anyway!" Keeping that gem of wisdom in mind, I wrote this little poem which I entitled.....

The Beginner

Smile when your golf ball smiles at you,
A shank or a whiff is no cause to be blue.
We're out here for fresh air and vitamin D,
And an underused word, camaraderie.

Check out the flowers and just look around;
Forget that your tee shot may never be found.
The course is so peaceful, the lake so serene;
Who cares it's a one iron to carry the green?

Look on the bright side, it's just a sand trap;
It could be Death Valley, and you with no map.
Don't worry, perhaps you'll be out of there soon;
It's eleven fifteen... yeah... most likely by noon!

Well, you finally got on and you're ready to putt;
Don't let those "butterflies" gnaw at your gut.
There really is no such a thing as the "yips;"
It's just a slight twitch of your wet fingertips.

That putting stance is an unusual sight;
Could it be your shorts are a little too tight?
Just hole that two incher, you'll be in the cup;
Great putt!.... That does it, now let's add it up.

That's right.... a 29's usually a fantastic score,
But for nine holes, not one.... we've got seventeen more!
We'd better move on, there's a foursome behind;
It looks like the **big** guy is losing his mind;
They're yelling and screaming, and one's turning blue;
Do you think there's a chance that they
wanna play through??

C'mon, ease up....
I never claimed to be Longfellow!...... hmmm

On the shores of Gitcherwallet,
By the shining Big-Sur-water;
Search the victims of the ice plant,
Guardian of the shank, the ice plant....

I'm sorry Henry.... lie still!

Chapter Two

Just A Little History

HISTORICAL NONSENSE

I never liked history. The better portion of my encounter with Western Civilization at the University of Arkansas was spent looking out the window at the beautiful maple trees on the lawn of the "Old Main" building, thinking about the golf course and how to fix my hook.

Other than possibly a direct descendent or an heir, who really gives a rat's backside what Attila the Hun or Charlemagne were doing forty thousand years ago, especially when you've got a golf match with the Texas Longhorns tomorrow and your putting needs work! Nasty old Attila never fought anybody as frightening as the "yips!" If he had ever tried to putt at Oakmont, he'd never have made the history books because he would still be there trying to negotiate those greens. He probably would have stampeded a few thousand horses over them just for spite!

Don't ever ask what I made in Western Civ.... thankfully, that is one subject I only have to deal with when playing Trivial Pursuit, which is about every three years at Christmas. However, as I continue on my average learning curve of getting one day smarter for every two days older, I'm beginning to see the wisdom in the old saying that goes, "In order to know where we are and where we're going, it's important to know where we've been."

Golf has been around about twice as long as the good old U.S.A., and if we're not careful, it might survive us. Luckily for us, the Japanese love golf, too. When they ultimately win the war by buying the United States, I hope they'll let us have a few tee times. They really are fanatical about the game. My father is a doctor and was in the Navy, stationed in Yokosuka, Japan, in the middle fifties. How vividly I remember going with him to a golf course near Tokyo and seeing about thirty women on their hands and knees, crawling down one of the fairways, pulling out every blade of undesirable grass. As you probably know, Japanese women treat their men very, very well.... at least they used to. Being only ten years old at the time, I didn't appreciate what I was witnessing. Those gals might have been the members' wives. Only in a wonderfully advanced society would the women make such a sacrifice so their husbands could enjoy a perfectly manicured course. I can just picture such a sight at the Houston Country Club! Please ladies.... I'm only teasing! There's not a chauvinistic bone in my body.... honest!

The Russians aren't much into the game yet, even though they now have a course in Moscow. If they ever get aggressive again and take over, we could perhaps forget about golf and start thinking about mining salt in Siberia. Maybe Karsten Solheim could start making little lightweight sledgehammers that range from C-7 to D-2 and go P-I-N-G! Call them the "NaCl Personal Model." Fortunately, there is the strong possibility that they might build a few more courses, get hooked on golf, and forget world conquest altogether! "Hey Nikita, are we going to attack in the morning?" "Nyet, cancel the missles for tomorrow, we've got an eight o'clock tee time at Cypress Pointzke." Wouldn't that be the ultimate joke! Eighty trillion dollars we've spent on nuclear weapons and all we needed to do was send over our old hickory shafted golf clubs and some "featherie" golf balls. I'd like to see how long it would take them to close that gap! Maybe that's what happened to communism. They started watching the Masters on TV and decided they wanted a little of the "good" life!

Forgive me... I was about to lose it altogether. I'm not in the mood to get serious, but I'll try.... shortly. This same problem haunted me in W. Civ.. Every time I'd open that book, it would only take about two sentences and my mind would be off on some wonderful little excursion. Honestly, I could sometimes read ten pages and not remember a single word. Don't leave me.... if I can have a little fun this history stuff is easier for me to get through.

I'm not totally certain what swing mechanics were like at the point in golf's history when a good stick and a "sheep chip" were the tools of the trade, but I've got a pretty good mental picture. Finding a "dry" chip was probably more important than how you swung at it. "Two!".... would have been a more appropriate warning for an errant shot than "fore!" Shooting at an associate or an animal was perhaps the original objective of the game. I can see the stats now. "Today I hit three shepherds and eleven sheep in regulation." Sounds like more fun to me! For certain it was less frustrating. Since that time however, dignity and decorum have prevailed, and mankind has proven his ingenuity and intelligence by pouring literally billions of dollars (easily enough to have fed everyone on earth who has starved to death since golf began) into what started as a harmless and affordable pastime. Not only that, he has made a science of it as well! Admittedly, yours truly included.

Well, what the heck! Who can think about world hunger when their golf ball is headed for a water hazard or an OB stake at the first hole? If you're lucky enough to be playing Augusta, who could think about the rest of the world — period? That's not to infer that those "wonderfully fortunate stalwarts of businessdom" (hereinafter shortened to lucky s.o.b.'s), are not concerned about global affairs. In fact, many times while strolling down the fairway of some gorgeous country club, I myself have wondered with deep consternation what might be happening in the rest of the world.... then I came to my next shot and promptly forgot about it! Truthfully, if you're playing Augusta or Cypress Point, it is so breathtaking that the rest of creation does indeed seem distant. Honest to.... oops.... forgive me Father.... but heaven's going to have to go some to beat those two places. Here's hoping Alister MacKenzie and Bobby Jones are up there right now designing courses all over the place, even if my chances of playing them are leaning to the slim side.

Golf actually does embody many worthwhile qualities which should not be overlooked, as well as giving mankind a civilized arena in which to study himself. Anyone who has ever seen Doug Sanders or Tommy Bolt at a tournament knows that people are more interesting to watch than zoo animals. A golf course offers a haven of relaxation where one may, if he so chooses, harmlessly vent hostilities which might otherwise be released upon his neighbor. Although the game may provoke some folks to drink or swear, it keeps others off the streets, away from drugs, and generally out of mischief. Golf also creates a perfect setting to really get to know someone. An individual's true personality will surface on the golf course sooner or later. It never fails! Refrain from ever signing a business deal with anyone until you play golf with him first, unless of course you don't want him to know too much about you, either. Speaking of business deals, I am told that more are consummated on the golf course than anywhere else. Those deals often turn into new industry through which the employees can keep the economy going around (as well as creating enough income to pay their bosses' club dues). The game itself is a great economic stimulator, creating income for everyone from tee manufacturers to psychiatrists, to (fortunately) golf pros. And ultimately, the game provides a service that few things in the world can match, aside from death and poverty; that of doling out an occasional slice of humility to anyone brazen enough to think he has the whole world by the short hair. Gotcha!

DIFFERENT TYPES OF SWING

Here comes the real stuff.... pay attention. One of the more fascinating things about golf is the seemingly endless number of ways that golf shots can be played. Equally intriguing are the considerable variances in how the swing itself can be powered by the body. Over the years (about five centuries), several definitive types of golf swing have evolved. The confusing thing is that each swing type is powered differently, yet they all have produced extremely successful, winning players. To the untrained and even the trained eye as well, power sources within the body can be difficult to differentiate. This is especially true when they are used in combination. There are three basic sources in the body from which to power the golf swing, and sometimes those sources are used in combination. Either the legs, the shoulders and arms, or the hands and forearms, may be used independently or together.

THE FLIP

The hand and forearm swing, or as some instructors call it, the "centrifugal flip," is generally associated with older style players. Some examples of great players with this style swing would be Sam Snead, Bobby Jones and Julius Boros. Bear in mind that there are many wonderful players in each category. Naming all of them would only be confusing, especially since some overlap into other power source categories. Therefore, I'll only give a few examples of each style. With some understanding about what to look for, you'll begin to see the differences between players and can make up your own mind where they go. If you have the video tape, it would be a good idea to carefully study the segment on various swing types. It will help your understanding and appreciation of the GRAVITY swing.

The "centrifugal flip," is a very smooth and easy looking swing, characterized by a timed "throwing" of the hands through the impact area. There is no "separation" or "coil" between the upper and lower body as in the GRAVITY swing, but simply a turn onto the back leg during the takeaway, and a turn back onto the front leg during delivery. The right arm is kept in an "elbow down" position during the backswing and the hands are fully cocked at the completion of the takeaway. The swing is given momentum by the forward turn, but most of the power is actually applied by the hands and forearms at the point of the angular release of the wrists into impact. The clubface goes from open to shut very quickly through the impact area, and even though this swing can be a beautiful and graceful thing when executed by the right player, it can be a timing nightmare! Not only that, it requires a very strong set of hands and forearms to achieve much distance with this style. Women and most older men, trying to use the "centrifugal flip," are going to have a tough time "hitting it out of their shadows!"

The major reason for the evolution of this style was because of the torque in the old wooden or hickory shafted golf clubs. If you can find one of these clubs, take hold of the grip in one hand and the clubhead in the other, and give it a good twist. You will feel a considerable amount of "give" in the shaft. The high degree of torque generated in hickory shafts, requires the user to "throw" the clubhead from open to closed through impact in order to prevent the ball from going to the right (referring to a right-handed player).

Even though the "centrifugal flip" swing has the two edged sword of the third law of motion hanging over it because of applied force (the action/reaction law), its use was necessitated by the equipment of the time. The advent of steel and other new shaft materials has eliminated the need for this swing style.

41

MY HERO

The greatest example (living or dead) of the shoulder and arm swing is, of course, the fabulous Arnold Palmer. Go Arnie! God, I loved him when I was a kid. I still do. We're not but about fifteen years apart in age, and he was just beginning to make waves at the time in my life when I needed a role model. My father should have been my role model, but since he was a pathologist, and spent most of his days cutting up dead people and looking into a microscope, I turned to Arnold. I've always loved my father very much, but Arnie was my hero! He could do anything! I watched him play an exhibition match at Rosswood C.C., in Pine Bluff, Arkansas, in the early to middle sixties. The exact year escapes me, but a few things I saw that day will be etched in my memory forever. The ninth hole was a four hundred and fifty yard dogleg right par four, second shot over a large pond, trees solid on both sides of the fairway, tee to green. Arnie drills it into the right woods off the tee onto the bare dirt. He's two hundred twenty yards from the hole, has the spookiest lie you've ever seen, needs to bend it forty yards to the right and negotiate what looked like the Sequoia National Forest — not to mention having to clear the lake! I'd have still loved him if he had chipped it out. Not my man! "Gimme the one iron," he says to the caddie. Since this was no formal occasion, some slightly inebriated character pipes up.... "Aw, c'mon, if you pull this shot off, I'm goin home." Arnie laughs and inquires how far it is to the man's car. However, as he walks to the ball, a look reminiscent of King Kong having a bad day, comes over his face. Shirt tail out, frankfurter size fingers squeeze the oil out of the leather grip, muscles flex.... **BAM!!!** Woodpeckers scream, one lady faints, others are panting and fanning themselves, squirrels go every direction, and the ball.... you guessed it, **TWO feet from the hole!** Honest to God, I'll never forget that shot if I live to be a hundred. What.... did he make the putt??? How dare you ask such an insulting question! He could have glared at it and it would have jumped in by itself! Arnie was wonderful, still is. He loves golf more than any man I've ever met, and my life has been better for knowing him.

However, the impression that Arnold made on me as a youngster, was a mixed blessing. He definitely inspired me to pursue a career in golf, but it took another ten years (and several frustrating ones on the tour) to convince me that I did not have the physical strength to swing like him. We're not going to discuss my father's or my grandfather's disappointment at not seeing my name ever make it onto the laboratory door as Dr. David Lee! PA (Grandad).... if you can hear me up there in heaven... I'm a golf pathologist — OK? So give me a break! You got me started in this freaking game anyway! Sorry for the interruption.

The shoulder and arm swing is the most prevalent of all styles of golf swing today, and simply uses the lower body as a stabilizing framework while the upper body beats the stuffing out of the ball. Forgive me Arnie, but you know it's true. This type of swing perfectly exemplifies the carnal instinct that every individual who picks up a club for the first time possesses... **KILL!**

Only occasionally does an outstanding athlete like Arnold learn to compensate for the tremendous back-pressure which the shoulder and arm swing exerts against the body and the swing-plane. It takes an extremely dedicated individual to become a great player with this method. More often than not, swinging the club in this manner is ultimately limiting to the development of the golfer. Although one may possess the strength to swing the club with great speed through force alone, should some of that power serve to move the body, and subsequently the swing-plane out of position — it has all gone for nothing (remember the action/reaction law). **Only when strength is used in compliance with good physics principles, does it prove to be not only an asset, but a great advantage.** If you're thinking that Arnold hasn't done too badly by trying to murder the ball all these years, you are exactly right. The point is, that had Arnold enjoyed Jack's mechanics, he might have won five hundred golf tournaments, given his "heart size." The same statement could be equally applied to other players, like Snead, Hogan or Player. By the time you finish this book, see what you think.

THE PROPER WAY

The lower body swing, or as I call it, the GRAVITY swing, is fairly new when compared to other styles. It is quite possible that there were others before him, but I like to think of Byron Nelson as the father of what many call the modern golf swing. Jack Nicklaus is, without question, the epitome of this swing type. There are other great players that may look different doing their version of the GRAVITY swing, but it is powered exactly the same. Variations in appearance of this style are often dictated by the physical characteristics of the individual. One may be built top heavy, while the next is bottom heavy, or thin versus portly. Five top GRAVITY players who have their own unique "look" are Lee Trevino, Raymond Floyd, Chi-Chi Rodriguez, Miller Barber and Fred Couples.

What classifies a person as having a "pure GRAVITY swing," is a complete absence of "applied" force from the upper body during delivery. There are currently a large number of players who use the legs to predominately power the swing, yet utilize some degree of upper body force. "Pure GRAVITY players," or ones who use virtually **no** upper body, are at this point in time relatively rare compared to the entire golfing population. This is because of the subtleties involved in the mechanics of this swing style, which, incidentally, have caused the historical difficulties of learning and teaching it.

Without question, the GRAVITY swing is the most energy efficient way possible to swing a golf club — but can be the most frightening if you don't understand it. What unsettles the player when he or she is learning this method is that the "pick-up" of the golf ball at impact is totally incidental to the swing itself. In other words, there is no striking at, or attempting to hit the ball. It is simply, in the way. One needs a high degree of faith to learn to trust the GRAVITY swing, because it feels at first as if there is no control over what is happening.

By strict definition of the rules, the GRAVITY swing is illegal. The rules declare that the ball must be "fairly struck at." In my opinion, to fairly strike at something requires a muscular flexing. The GRAVITY swing is a timed whip, powered by rotary torque from the front leg (the mechanics will be explained in complete detail in chapter five), while the arms are simply going "along for the ride" and providing a connection to the club. The eminent Joe Dey once told me that every word in the rule book meant <u>exactly</u> what it said. Wouldn't it be a kick if they asked Jack and Lee to give back all the trophies and the money? Of course the wording should be changed to state "with the intent of moving the ball." I realize that such an observation is being nit-picky, and that there weren't many GRAVITY players around when they wrote the rules, but that's what it says.

Characteristic results of the GRAVITY swing are more solid, higher and straighter flying shots. GRAVITY players have the ability to move the ball with power, either right to left, or left to right. "Shoulder and arm" players, and "centrifugal flip" players, tend to have a predominant draw pattern caused by some degree of plane reversal (caused by <u>applied</u> upper body force), and have difficulty hitting a powerful shot that fades.

The only disadvantage of the GRAVITY swing is that if the player is doing something wrong, his pattern of mis-hits may not be predictable. Because of the passiveness in the arms, the ball may go left one time and right the next, if the swing is being "abused." Most GRAVITY players who abuse the swing through some degree of applied force, seldom become household names. Failure to understand the subtleties of this method, has prevented some very promising players from realizing their potential. When Byron Nelson was on his game, he was unbeatable; but when he was off, was known to be wild. The same problems occasionally haunt Ballesteros and Greg Norman, as well as Tom Watson, Ben Crenshaw and John Miller. This group of men are all GRAVITY players who get at least ninety percent of their power from the lower body. However, as you will soon learn, just **a little bit** of upper body force can send a 270 yard drive to a place where Dick Tracy couldn't find it. Failure to understand the GRAVITY swing and get it under complete control, drove two potentially fabulous players right off the tour—Tom Weiskopf and Marty Fleckman. They aren't the only examples by any means.

Getting the absolute most from this method is dependent on developing the proper mechanics and trusting the swing enough to "let it work for you." Why certain players (such as Nicklaus and Trevino) have learned to control it better than others, is largely a mystery—since their writings and instructional materials don't indicate that they fully understand it. They just "feel it" and trust it enough to "leave it alone." As a matter of fact, Nicklaus, in his early days, had periods when he let the swing get out of control by applying force to it. Improper manipulation of the swing (or trying to "guide" the ball) can be devastating, as you are about to discover.

The most wonderful thing about this method is that, once you understand how it works, it is very simple to teach yourself to use it effectively. All that's required is a little of your time and patience, and some **correct** practice. The knowledge that you are practicing properly, and not chasing shadows or dead ends, will motivate you to keep going until you reach whatever level you desire. The frustration of knowing or suspecting that you are practicing wrong can be overwhelming. How well I remember the many years and countless days I've gone to the practice tee, dumped my golf balls on the ground, and just stood over them for a few minutes wondering what I was going to try that day. Believe me, it was rarely the same thing twice. Unfortunately, I can't do anything about the practicing dilemmas you've suffered in the past, but that does not have to be the case in the future.

THE CONFUSING WAY

A discussion of the history and variations of swing types cannot be complete without discussing the "combination" swing. In this method, part of the power comes from the legs and part from the upper body. Some of the players who use it have had a profound effect on the game. Two players who have used a combination of upper and lower body power in the swing, to great success, are Ben Hogan and Gary Player. Nick Faldo and Larry Nelson are also good examples and there are many others.

The overall influence of Ben Hogan on the teaching of golf in the last forty years cannot be overstated. Hogan is well known for being one of the most disciplined practicers of all time. He had the grit and determination to rise above physical handicap and excel at golf as few men ever have. His influence on swing style, however (like Palmer's), has been a mixed blessing. From the positive side, he has been extremely inspirational to thousands of players, by demonstrating that "will" can prevail. On the other hand, even though his teachings embody (for the most part) solid fundamentals, there are some direct and important conflicts with good physics principles. In the chapter on drills, I will show you how to prove this to yourself.

By looking at the evolution of Hogan as a player, one can see how he developed some misconceptions of correct mechanics. In his early days he had the problem of swinging the club back too far in the takeaway. You can witness this backswing fault by looking at a copy of his first book titled "Power Golf." The reason for the club going back too far was an incorrect origin of takeaway. By starting the backswing with the hands, instead of the shoulders and back, the club passed through the twelve o'clock position so quickly, that it dropped below parallel (three o'clock) before he could complete his weight transfer back to his left side and start the delivery. Once the club drops below three o'clock in the backswing, it requires **considerable** tension in the arms to make the change of direction, and an early release into impact (which causes wildness) is usually the result. Hogan knew he shouldn't take the club back that far. He had a severe control problem in his early days and was determined to remedy it. However, instead of changing the origin of the takeaway totally to his shoulders and back, which would have brought the club through twelve o'clock slower — allowing him time to complete his weight transfer before the club dropped below parallel — he tucked and froze the right elbow against his body. By not allowing the right elbow to leave his side during the takeaway, he knew the club wouldn't drop below parallel because it would hit him in the back before it could. The result was that, by hinging the swing from the right elbow instead of the right shoulder (as Nicklaus does) Hogan solved the "over-swing" problem —

49

but lost about a foot in the overall diameter of the swing arc. What he lost in available leverage and club speed, by having a smaller arc, he had to make up for with an additional "hit" from the hands and arms through impact. Except for this characteristic, his swing is exactly like the true GRAVITY swing. It is however, an important variance. The applied force from the hands and arms is **not** in compliance with good physics principles, since it makes the player vulnerable to the action/reaction law, and is **not** required if the full available arc size is utilized. Although Hogan had the strength and determination to learn to compensate for the "back-pressure" to his swing-plane (caused by the hit from the hands and arms), the average player does not. It takes a player of great arm and hand strength to hit the ball any appreciable distance with this method. Women and older men are at a distinct disadvantage trying to use it.

THE IRONY

There is often considerable irony in the history and sequence of events. When Hogan released his second book, titled the "Five Fundamentals of Modern Golf," the golf world was at a very vulnerable point. Admirers, worldwide, had watched Hogan come back from a near fatal auto accident in 1949 to compile a fantastic tournament record — while literally dragging his legs behind him. Even after having been told that he would never walk again, he was determined to play winning golf, and did. The mystery of what made Ben Hogan "tick" was even more dramatized by the fact that he had very little to say to anyone. Not only was the world waiting anxiously to know what drove him, it wanted to know how he hit the ball so straight. When "Five Fundamentals" was released in the middle fifties, golfdom snatched it up like a hundred dollar bill laying on the sidewalk. The book instantly became the golf "bible" of instruction, and for thousands of players and professionals, still is today.

Here's the most ironic part of all. When Jack Nicklaus came along in the early sixties and started winning everything in sight, concessions to his technique came slowly and begrudgingly. Analysts said, "well Jack.... you obviously hit the ball farther than anyone.... higher, more solid, sometimes straighter. There's no doubt you're beating everyone, including our beloved Arnie. Your swing is smooth and fluid, and your balance is not so bad. Aside from that ridiculous crew cut and a few extra pounds.... oh!... and that squeaky little voice that wouldn't fit any macho sports jock, there's only one thing wrong.... that "flying" right arm has got to go. Ben Hogan says that's wrong." Hardly anyone considered that perhaps Jack's technique was correct, and that Hogan's should have been the one in question. There's a lot to be said for getting your two cents in first. After Hogan wrote the "bible" and handed down the commandment, "Thou shalt keep thy right elbow tucked," Jack didn't stand much of a chance in the "swing authority" category, regardless of how well he played. Jack's position as an instructor hasn't been aided by the fact that he fails to have a totally clear picture of how his own technique works, or just how good it really is. Trying to learn the GRAVITY swing from his books or video tapes is like taking a course in adjectives and gray terms. He says, "the swing has got to have timing, rhythm, grace and fluid movement." That's like telling someone that to set a world record in the high jump, you just have to jump higher than anyone else, or to dance like Michael Jackson, you just have to wiggle.

In defense of Jack (not that he needs it), the more energy efficient the swing becomes, the more subtle it becomes, and the more difficult it is to explain to someone else. One of the best ways to learn from Jack's video tapes, not that cybernetics is the answer (but it doesn't hurt), is to turn the sound down and simply watch him swing, over and over again. After a while, you'll start to get a feel for the unique rhythm. In this book, however, you will learn a much better way to instill a perfect swing in your body, and prove to yourself in the process that golf has been taught **totally backwards** for hundreds of years.

THE TOUGH PART OF TEACHING

One of the great weaknesses in the teaching of golf, is that instructors have been historically reluctant to flatly state that one mechanical style is superior to another. The reasons for this are several. For one, **it is often difficult to see where quality of the technique ends and the perseverance of the individual begins,** and as mentioned previously, there are indeed more factors that determine a great player than just mechanics. Another reason could be that the gentlemanly nature of the game might be violated by criticism, even though it were constructive. Hogan was obviously a man of superior determination and without question should be admired for it. However, when one is looking for a swing style to imitate, his would not be the wisest choice according to mother nature and the laws of motion.

The objective of this book is not to compare "race horses," but to define through logic and good physics, what mechanical principles will repeat most consistently — given that other factors such as "heart size" and determination are equal. In fact, confidence and determination can grow out of the knowledge that one's mechanics are correct and that practice time is not being wasted.

Rest assured that when I make the statement—from a physics standpoint—that Nicklaus, Trevino and Miller Barber have better golf swings than Hogan or Snead, I will explain to you exactly why that is, and why it would ultimately improve your golf if you can employ their mechanics in your body. In **no** way am I inferring that they were necessarily better players. Obviously, Miller Barber's tournament record pales in the shadow of Hogan's or Snead's. For the record, **Jack** is, in my opinion, the finest player, with the best swing, of anyone who has ever played the game. There.... I said it!

Tiptoeing over the hot coals of player comparisons is never a task I enjoy, especially when all the players mentioned (regardless of their technique) have played better than yours truly. However, for you to know that you are getting the best possible information, it needs to be done. It always rankles me when someone says, "David, if you're so all-fired intelligent, why haven't you won the U.S. Open? Those who can... do, those who can't... teach." Normally, my reply is a reminder that were it not for guys like me, who would mend the awful golf swings like theirs? Do they think Jack is going to be available for personal lessons? It has taken a lifetime of diligent study to discover and understand the things that are revealed in this book, and I believe beyond a shadow of a doubt that had I understood them twenty years ago, my life as a tournament player would have been entirely different. Like thousands of others, I was just one more player that almost made it, but couldn't quite get over the edge. It would be easy to look back and claim ignorance and lack of discipline as excuses, but my lack of discipline was largely brought on by the knowledge that I didn't have a clue as to what I was doing. Had the book that you are holding been in my hands a few years ago, I would have had **no** reason for failing to become a great player other than lack of desire — which wasn't my problem. What you are about to read can make the "size of your heart" the only limiting factor in your golf development. The price I've paid to transcend mechanical golf is one that you can avoid — and believe me, the cost can be high. I've got a trail of ex-wives and too many fast food dinners to prove it. You will **still have to train your body** to make the swing properly; but you need not go through a lifetime of chasing one dead end after another. **Ingraining poor mechanics in your system will only allow you to develop to a certain level, and then it is like hitting a brick wall. It seems almost impossible to get any better. You cannot employ a swing that, from a physics standpoint, is a slap in the face of mother nature every time you make it. Even though the lady may tease you with occasional good shots, she will turn on you sooner or later. Believe it!**

You are about to learn that parts of your brain which you take totally for granted.... can teach you to hit a golf ball as well as your heart desires. All you have to do is wake them up. Exactly how to do that will soon be revealed to you. Your amazing mind will do the rest.

I'm still not crazy about history.....

Chapter Three

Equipment

WOW!

Space balls! XLR4219 heads and laser tested graphite, boron and plutonium alloy shafts. My God.... they've gone crazy! Going to the PGA merchandise show nowadays is wilder than EPCOT center. Simply trying to read a catalog from one of the major manufacturers can give you a headache, if not a severe case of confusion. There are so many clubs to choose from and all of them promise to make you hit it farther, straighter, get more backspin, and look better doing it. TV commercials tempt us. Try our new ball, the XLLLLD. Carry the Mediterranean Sea! Seriously, what are the real facts? Farther? A little. Straighter? A little. More backspin? A little. The dent in your wallet? **A lot!** Guaranteed to make you hit it like Greg Norman? **Not likely!**

It is true that modern technology has made considerable strides with new shaft materials and that perimeter weighted clubheads are more forgiving to mis-hit shots. The newest shaft materials do indeed have less torque, which reduces clubhead twisting at impact. Some of the newer shafts respond faster, which along with being lighter, allows for an increase in clubhead speed and subsequently greater distance. However, even with all this going for us, these advancements are relatively insignificant when compared to the importance of proper technique. Don't forget that the rules of golf are limiting to equipment design. The rules state that a tournament legal golf ball must travel only so fast, and that tournament legal clubs must be built within certain specifications. This is to ensure that skill is not lost as the basis of the game and to prevent courses from becoming obsolete.

Everyone wants the latest clubs on the market and isn't it exciting to get a new set? Although the cosmetics of equipment are more glamorous today, a new set of "sticks" was just as wonderful to me in 1955 as it is now. In fact more so. You used to get a fancy box with a slot for each club, but once you took them out, they were hell to put back. Nowadays you don't get a box. Just "grab em" off the rack and go! Your first set of "pro line" clubs is always the most exciting! "Now I can break par for sure!" Right Ralph! Over the past thirty-five years I've had enough new clubs that the excitement has worn a little thin, but hope for that "perfect set" springs eternal. Isn't it a pain that there is always one club in a set that doesn't look or feel quite right? It never fails! No manufacturer in his right mind would make a perfect set this year knowing that he had to bring out a new model to get any sales next year. Every time a new model comes out, we are told it is the "ultimate" golf club. They should be reminded that if this year's model is the ultimate, then next years will have to be the "ultimater," and the year after that.... well?

WE'RE LIMITED

I'd like to give you a perfect example of how stringent the rules are on club specifications and how little they have actually changed since the advent of the steel shaft. In about 1986, Wilson Sporting Goods released a "top of the line" model of irons, that was nearly a dead ringer for a gooseneck model they had put on the market forty years ago. Hardly anyone has seen the originals in twenty years, so who would know the difference? But today they're the "state of the art." "Horse feathers!"

All these "wonderful strides" in equipment mean very little unless the monkey on the other end of the stick knows how to swing. There are plenty of guys who could take just one club and beat the average player. Lee Trevino could whip a fair percentage of the golf world by playing with just a Coke bottle! If you don't believe it, bring your wallet!

None of this is to say that there are not important things you should consider when purchasing a set of clubs.

BE CAREFUL WHEN YOU BUY!

There are several factors to consider preceding the purchase. Incidentally, should someone give you an old set that has been sitting around the attic or garage for twenty or thirty years because a spouse passed away or gave up the game, don't disdain the gift until you know what you've got. The clubs may (though usually unbeknown to the giver) be very valuable. There are many older clubs that are considered to be classics as well as collectors' items. Be wary if, for example, you are trading in an old set of MacGregor woods, of the crafty pro who is too eager to make you an "offer you can't refuse" on a new set. You may well be trading in clubs that, even though they may be dusty and need refinishing, are not only technically superior, but much more valuable than the ones you are interested in purchasing. The trader walks off thinking he has gotten a great deal and the pro tiptoes away "licking his chops." For the right Ben Hogan MacGregor driver, you could get an entire set of new graphite shafted woods and irons, bag and putter thrown in for "good will" — and you might <u>still</u> be getting the short end of the deal. The bottom line is; if you have old clubs laying around the house, don't unload them in a garage sale for twenty bucks until you check them out.

WEIGHT

When selecting a new set, one of the first considerations is to choose the correct overall weight for your build and swing. A golf club should neither be too heavy, nor too light. In today's equipment, there is a strong movement toward making clubs lighter. This is to allow the player to generate more clubhead speed and to handle the club more easily. However, there is a point of diminishing return to consider. One primary function of the golf club is to act as a balancing agent for the swing, much in the same way a balance pole does for a tightrope walker. The objective is to provide enough resistance through overall club weight, to allow the player something to "hold onto" for the sake of balance during the swing. The balancing pole, because of it's resistance to movement, serves the tightrope walker as an object which he can pull against to stabilize his balance. The walker about to go across Niagra Falls on a wire would be less than impressed by the "helpful" individual who might suggest that he could handle the pole more easily by cutting five feet from either end. Making a golf club too light can be self defeating, since the potential gain of increased clubhead speed and greater distance can be more than offset by a loss of balance due to decreased club resistance. The woeful result can often be mis-hit and off-line shots. Likewise, a club that is too heavy may cause the player to labor, and perhaps once again throw himself off balance. Also, if the club is too heavy, the player will experience a decrease in clubhead speed and a loss of distance. There is an optimum overall club weight and swingweight for every golfer, and it will ultimately help your development and caliber of play to find the correct weights for your build. When I have a set of clubs built, my personal tendency is to have the swingweights set about two points lighter than I intend for them to ultimately be. When I take them to the practice tee for the first time, I will then bring them up to ideal weight with a few strips of lead tape placed on the back of each clubhead. This way I can get each club to "feel" just right. There is a correct head weight to shaft flex ratio for the club to transmit maximum sensitivity to the player. Shafts will vary slightly in their feel, and it is rare to pre-order a supposedly desired swingweight and have each club come out feeling perfect. It is easier to add a little lead tape, to bring the weight up (should the clubhead feel too light for the shaft), than it is to grind the head down if it feels too heavy. As most golfers know, pros are habitual users of lead tape on their clubs, and although it doesn't look too nice on the back of a new club, it does work well. If for no other reason, you might instill a little fear in your playing partners by putting a strip or two on the back of your sticks, thereby leading them to think you know what you're doing.

LENGTH

Club length is an important factor to consider. The proper length should be determined by the distance your fingertips are from the floor when standing upright with arms relaxed. That distance for the average male and female, regardless of overall height, will be about 29 and 28 inches respectively. Industry "standards" for club lengths are determined by these measurements. If your fingertips are farther from the floor than these distances, you may need longer clubs with more upright lies. Should your fingertips be closer to the floor, you may not need shorter clubs, but simply flatter than standard lies. Because this book is not a club fitting manual, it is not in anyone's interest to go into this area too deeply, especially since I am not sizing a set for you. Just remember that club length and lie are important, and any good professional should be able to fit you in this regard. By the way, before you run out and buy yourself a forty-six inch driver thinking you are going to hit the ball farther, consider this. There is a reason they don't normally make drivers fifty inches or more in length, even though a player might hit the ball a greater distance with such a club if he could connect properly with the ball. Again, the point of diminishing return tells us that approximately forty-three inches of driver length for the average male is about all he can handle with consistent results.

LIE

Club lie (page 61, fig. A), especially to the GRAVITY player with passive hands, is very important. If your clubs are

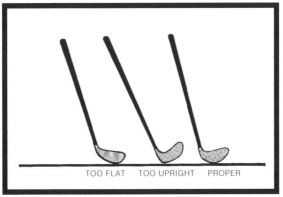

Fig. A Club Lie Comparison

too flat, the ball will have a tendency to go to the right, and if they are too upright, it will go to the left unless compensating measures are taken. For your set to be correct, when you are at a comfortable and proper address position, the toe of the club should sit slightly off the ground when soled (check them on a hard surface). This allows for the downward deflection of the club

Fig. B Shaft Deflection

shaft during the swing (Fig. B), caused by centrifugal force and the resulting leverage of the offset clubhead against the shaft.

SHAFT FLEX

Shaft flex is another considerable point. If the shaft is too stiff, the club has a tendency to get to the ball too soon in the swing, causing a painful stinging sensation in the hands, as well as a loss of feel in the shot. Should the shaft be too flexible, it will lag considerably during the swing and a loss of control may result.

There are so many shafts on the market today that it is difficult, as well as impractical, for me to make a recommendation. Many of the new materials are excellent and would undoubtedly work for you. It is much a matter of preference. I've been using the True Temper dynamic steel shaft for years and it is a tried and tested shaft which many professionals use. There have been a jillion tournaments won with dynamic shafts. That is not to say that my mind is closed and that next week you might not see me playing with graphite. Most good golf shops have demo clubs and you can see what feels best to you.

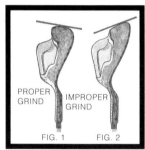

Fig. C Camber Angles

CAMBER

There is another factor that should not be forgotten when buying a set of irons. The **camber** on the sole of the club is **very** important (see fig. C). This is one of the most critical features of an iron club, and one that is often overlooked and improperly designed by many manufacturers. On most shots, an iron club should cut the turf like a cheese knife. In other words, it should allow the player to easily take a divot with his shot, but not cut the ground so deeply that he might risk hurting his hands or wrists. If you study the diagram, you will see in figure 1, how the club should be properly ground across the sole. When swinging a club designed in this manner, the rider flange will deflect the club from digging too deeply. A club designed as in figure 2, will actually suck itself into the ground if the angle of descent in the swing-plane is a little too steep. Some golf clubs are really dangerous to the user in this regard. If you are taking big "chunky" divots, look at your clubs carefully and see if they are cambered properly. This is especially important if you live or play in an area where the soils have a high clay content. Clay soils have a tendency to "grab" the clubhead if the blade is a "digger," and you can rattle your teeth loose if you're not careful. Many, many players have ruined or injured their hands and wrists using improperly cambered irons.

GRIPS

Grips are, once again, a matter of personal preference. Leather grips generally have a good feel to them, but can be rough on the hands, as well as expensive and more difficult to maintain. The plain rubber "victory" grip is one of the best ever made, and they are simple to care for. After a little oil and grime builds up on them, they wash easily and feel almost like new again. Grip size is important, because your hands will be more difficult to "cinch" onto the club consistently if your grips are either too large or too small. If you think you need a variation from standard grip size, get your professional to help you special order them, or let him fix them for you. It is not too frequent that an individual need vary from standard, but in some cases it is necessary and will help.

Now then, after you've spent part of your child's college fund on new clubs and still can't break 100, keep reading and discover that swinging it properly is far more important than how the club looks, or the materials from which it is made. The best players could take the worst clubs and still break 80. The score advantage between the finest, most expensive clubs on the market, and the cheapest pieces of junk, would be — at best — possibly ten strokes. That obviously is not to say that equipment is not of primary importance, but simply to point out that correct technique can take you from shooting 120, all the way to par or below. Good clubs will definitely take some of the sting out of a bad shot, but <u>fortunately</u> will not make you a great player. If that were the case, they would be much more expensive than they already are, and only the rich folks would be any good. Golf is an ultimately fair game! Remember also, Bobby Jones shot some pretty great scores with hickory shafted clubs, and without XLLLLD golf balls.

Chapter Four

The Grip

It's time to ease off the humor and get down to business. If we're going to hit it anywhere close to Greg Norman.... that's sort of funny in itself.... it is imperative that we know how to "grab hold" of the club correctly.

HOW TO GET A PERFECT GRIP

When the club is held properly, a secure grip can be maintained without having tension in the wrists or forearms. This is very important because the ability to achieve maximum clubhead speed through the impact area is dependent on the ability to make an unrestricted (by tension) release of the fully cocked wrists through impact. Should the club be placed too much in the palm of either hand, tension goes through the wrists in the process of securing the grip. When the club is gripped in a cinching fashion, in the fingers, tension does not go through the wrists,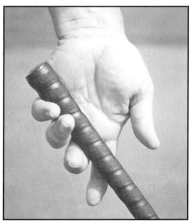

Photo A

making it possible to achieve an unrestricted release through impact, while maintaining a firm hold on the club.

Beginning with the left hand (right handed player), this is accomplished by placing the club at the base of the palm (photo A), against the pads of the last three fingers. The fingers should gently stretch, then close around the club, while the palm is pulled up from the fingers and then cinched down snugly. **This cinching action automatically tightens the grip without putting tension through the wrist.** The base of the left thumb should be retracted toward the body, and the first knuckle from the end of the thumb, should push down gently against the shaft, while the second knuckle of the thumb snaps down like a pair of vise pliers. This is called a short thumb position (photo B).

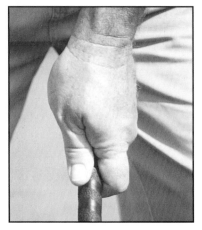

Photo B

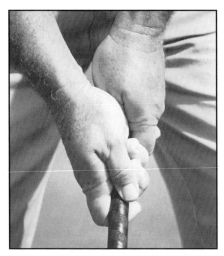

Photo C

The left hand and wrist, when properly placed on the club, should be approximately 30 degrees to the right of

66

vertical wrist axis position. The V of the left hand should point generally toward the right side of your neck.

Photo D

The same cinching action is done with the two middle fingers of the right hand (photo D). The pad at the base of the right thumb holds the left thumb securely in place.

The tip of the right thumb and the tip of the right index finger should either touch, or almost touch, depending on the size of the individuals hands.

Photo E

The little finger of the right hand should interlock with the index finger of the left hand (photo E). In my opinion, the interlocking grip allows the hands to function more easily as a single unit. When the interlocking grip is used, the right hand is in a more secure position, with more of it on the club than in the Vardon or overlapping grip.

Using the baseball grip, where all the fingers of both hands are on the club, places the hands a little too far apart. This tends to cause a flipping action as the club comes into the impact area. The baseball grip is fine for children with very small hands, but should be changed to an interlocking grip as they get older.

The cinching effect, created by stretching the palms from the fingers before closing the hands, ensures a secure, powerful grip, **without having to physically squeeze** the club with the hands. I've never agreed with the suggestion that the club should be held like a small bird. Holding the club too loosely, causes an involuntary tightening of the grip during the takeaway and upon delivery, which results in tension coming into the wrists, and a subsequent reduction in clubhead speed. A more correct feeling of grip pressure would be likened to holding a small rattlesnake behind the head. Allow him to breathe, but be darn sure he doesn't get away. The finished and proper grip is shown in photo C.

When the backswing reaches the point of first release (see next chapter for full explanation), after the arms have moved about twelve inches into the takeaway, even though the tension comes completely out of the wrists and arms, **the grip on the club does not loosen, because the hands were cinched onto the club when the grip was taken. The ability to maintain a secure grip throughout the swing, even though the forearms and wrists have totally relaxed at the point of first release, is critical to the success of the shot.**

Assuming the clubface is square to the intended flightline, and that ball position, alignment and swing sequencing are correct, if the grip is overly strong (hands rotated too much to the right [right handed player]), the ball will hook, or pull, to the left. The opposite will occur if the grip is too weak (hands rotated too far to the left). When a player takes his grip incorrectly, then makes an "in swing" compensation, either voluntary or involuntary, the desired ball flight pattern may, but often does not occur. Making swing compensations for a faulty grip rarely produces consistent results. **The ability of any player to hit quality, repeating shots, is first dependent on having a good grip. Usually, the better the player, the better the grip.**

WHAT HAPPENS IF WE DON'T

An incorrect, or insecure grip, can trigger **devastating** subconscious reactions in the mind of the player during the golf swing. If the grip is placed on the club in too strong a position, causing the ball flight pattern to be to the left, the player will normally develop a tendency to make "in swing" corrections, either consciously or subconsciously. Should the golfer "chase" the desired flight line in an effort to make the ball go there, he will have to do so with his own physical strength, and in the process, will put some degree of back-pressure against the swing-plane. Unless this back-pressure and the resulting plane reversal is compensated for, a mis-hit shot will occur.

As can easily be seen, a domino effect of compensations may begin to occur. Example: Too strong a grip, ball goes left.... player physically tries to block hook, unintentionally reverses swing-plane and hits ball fat, etc., etc.. Get the idea? The subconscious mind will try to make compensations for anything it senses may be wrong in the swing, regardless of whether or not those corrections are based on solid mechanical principles. One can easily become so mired in a series of incorrect compensations, **starting with, and triggered by a faulty grip,** that it is difficult to ever "dig out of the hole." If we learn to hold the club correctly in the beginning, it is much easier to develop a properly functioning golf swing which is free of compensations. In fact, a totally efficient swing is unlikely to occur unless the grip is correct. Once we know how to hold the club properly, learning to swing the club with realistic expectations that the ball will go on line, is far less complicated. However, even with the advantage that we now have a correct grip, there are a few other details to consider before we hit the ball like Jack....

Chapter Five

Mechanics of the "Gravity" Swing

When I finish writing this chapter, the rest of my life should seem like a soft Caribbean breeze. I've been procrastinating on this one for a long time, not for a lack of understanding, but because of the complexity of offering an easily understood picture of all the required movements. There is an overwhelming desire to put all the information on one line, thereby giving the reader a concise mental picture of everything that happens during the swing. However, that is obviously impossible in the written word. Every mechanical movement must be described in detail, and the reader required to commit each one to memory and paste them all together at the end. Instant headache! Fortunately, the next chapter tells you how to do everything you are going to learn in this chapter, without having to think about it. Just one of the advantages of learning golf through this system is that **by practicing the drills that are described in chapter six, a totally efficient and properly functioning GRAVITY swing can be learned without any required understanding of the mechanics that are about to be explained.** However, any golfer will ultimately gain both confidence and satisfaction from knowing how his swing works, as well as the ability to identify the **root** problem, if something is not functioning properly.

One of the most common and unintentional mistakes of many golf professionals and well intentioned amateurs "helping" their friends is to work on the areas of the swing that are obviously wrong, while many times overlooking the fundamental cause or flaw which precipitates a glaring error later in the movement. Obviously, it is preferable to treat the disease rather than the symptom.

START IT CORRECTLY

By the time the arms have moved approximately twelve inches in the takeaway, the domino that triggers a sequentially correct swing has already fallen. If the swing isn't started properly, a backlash of improper tension relationships between the body parts occurs and, unless compensations are made, the desired result for the shot will not be achieved. Even if all the mistakes are compensated for and the result comes off as planned, the energy efficiency level will not be at its highest potential and the odds of consistency in subsequent shots are diminished. **The more energy expended to produce a swing, the greater the likelihood that the body will be thrown off balance and the swing-plane forced out of kilter.**

HOLD EVERYTHING

Let me not get ahead of myself. Many of the things I will ask you to do in chapter six are different than the traditional approach to learning golf. **It is the absolute truth when I tell you that a total beginner can be trained to a par level player in as little as twelve to eighteen months with this method.** Even knowing that, there are many people who would not willingly try the techniques we use without the fundamental reasoning behind the concepts being convincing enough to make them overcome their pre-conceived notions of how golf should be learned. There are also many folks who, because of their resistance to change and their tenacity for tradition, would probably have reluctance toward doing some of the things I will ask you to do — even if Jack Nicklaus was standing on the practice tee telling them they should. There was a period in my life when that would have bothered me. It doesn't any longer. If you want to keep practicing your mistakes thinking that someday they will go away, this is America and you are entitled. If, however, you are tired of working hard on your golf swing — **only to see yourself stuck at the same level you've been for years** — or if you see yourself getting worse, or if you are not developing at a rate you think appropriate — consider the following possibilities and circle any appropriate letters.

    A. You are too uncoordinated to learn.
    B. You are not bright enough to learn.
    C. You can't find time to practice.
    D. You are practicing bad things.
    E. You get too much contradictory information and can't decide how much of it is valid and what you should really be practicing.
    F. The things you discover that work seem to do so only for a short while and then they go away.

If you circled any letters other than D, E and F, you are suffering from a lack of self confidence and discipline. Assuming you circled D, E and F, you're right in the same boat

73

with 99% plus of the entire world golfing community. Why do you suppose that so many people, touring pros included, struggle with the mechanics of their golf swings? From my perspective, the problem reflects the enormous subtleties and the complexity of controlling the human body in such a demandingly precise activity. Once in a while we "stumble" across it, but consistent repetition can be very elusive.

My preference, preceeding a discussion of mechanics, or a golf lesson, is to ask a series of deductive questions. Try this: Ask yourself and everyone you know who plays golf, to describe in as few words as possible what they feel when they hit a "perfect" golf shot. In a time when it is difficult to find five people who will agree on anything, almost invariably the answer will come back, "when I hit it perfectly, I don't feel anything." Or they'll say "it feels good," which is saying practically the same thing. Occasionally someone claims that the feeling is "orgasmic." Either they hit the ball better than I do, or their sex life is a lot worse. Nevertheless, take your own poll and you'll be amazed at the consistency of response. What's more, the answers are correct. When a golf ball is struck properly, there is not a lot of sensation other than exhilaration, a sense of balance and a solid smacking sound. What these universal answers really mean, is that the body has experienced a high level of efficiency of movement. Everything moves in harmony and nothing labors. Unfortunately, this is where the nightmare and frustration begin. When a player makes what for him is a perfect swing, the first thing that usually goes through his mind while he's standing there posing in the follow-through is "WOW!.... what did I do?" Then when he turns around and tries to "make" it happen, it won't work. Instant heartache! **The problem is, that the**

level of subtlety in a totally efficient swing is so enormous, that it is extremely difficult to pinpoint the exact things that cause it to occur. The "catch 22" for me as an instructor, is that I can't just tell my students to go out and practice until they don't "feel anything," and yet for them to achieve a level of totally efficient mechanics, that is exactly the task before me. Can I do that for you? **Absolutely!** In fact, after you read this book, and especially the next chapter, **you can do it all by yourself.**

Let's begin right here and explain how the GRAVITY swing works. Remember, even though the mechanics are complex, it is not necessary to understand them in order for you to learn properly. Truthfully, you could skip this chapter and still learn how to hit the ball exactly like Jack Nicklaus. However, it will ultimately help your ability to analyze the swing (both your own and others), if you understand how it should function. The confidence you'll gain from knowing that you are practicing properly will help you discipline yourself to get out there. This explanation is dedicated to every little kid like me who took his dad's watch apart to see what made it tick, and then moved on to the much more complex mechanism known as the golf swing.

Here goes: Incidentally, the swing is being explained from a **right-hander's** point of view. You southpaws are used to having to flip-flop everything anyway.

THE ORIGIN OF THE TAKEAWAY

The proper origin of takeaway in the GRAVITY swing is the back and shoulders. After a proper grip is taken (chapter 4) and the ball placed in the correct position relative to the feet for the type of shot desired, the arms and shoulders should extend downward and flex sufficiently to allow the **back and shoulders** to start the swing in **"one piece."** As the swing begins, the shoulders, arms and club, should retain the same relative positions they had at the start. Initiating the takeaway with the arms and hands totally relaxed, will set you into motion like a snake, with the shoulders getting ahead of the hands, which is not good. Weight distribution should be comfortably balanced between the heels and the balls of the feet, with the hip muscles carrying most of the weight load. Reference chapter eight, page 151 for stance width variations

Photo A

from shot to shot and with various clubs. If too much flex in the knees occurs in the set-up, the quadriceps above the knees load, and proper rotary motion in the delivery is restricted. One should feel "light" on the feet with a sense of mobility. In a full swing, a rhythmical rocking motion from foot to foot during address will facilitate an easier start to the takeaway and will aid subsequent key elements in the swing. Being "frozen" at address, creates tension problems and subsequent timing errors in the swing.

The tempo of the GRAVITY swing is in four beats. It is fast (powerful), slow, slow, fast. As we go along, I'll elaborate on each area.

THE HEAVE

In order to achieve maximum clubhead speed and control, **it is critical to start the backswing with a back and shoulder movement that is powerful enough to allow ALL OF THE TENSION in the wrists, arms, and shoulders, to fully release by the time the arms and club reach a point approximately at the seven-thirty position** when the body is viewed like a clock from the facing position (see photo A, page 76).... long sentence, deep breath.... **and yet for the arms and shoulders to be able to complete the backswing without ANY lift from the hands and arms beyond the seven-thirty point.** Read the last sentence at least twice more. If tension in the arms or shoulders remains beyond the seven-thirty point, timing in the swing is thrown off and the body will be pulled into a sway, or else the brain will sense the sway coming and freeze the weight transfer. Either way, trouble starts. My preference is to call the start of the takeaway a **"heave,"** simply because the tension which allows the swing to start in one piece must be literally thrown out of the arms. It is a move made with the back, very akin to the way one would throw a "medicine" ball. None of my students like the word "heave," and frankly I don't either, but I have yet to come up with a better descriptive term for the way the takeaway begins.

Don't confuse yourself by thinking that a powerful start in the first movement (or heave) will make the backswing look fast. It is simply powerful. If you have ever tried to pick up a long board from one end and move it laterally, you know that because of the leverage resistance caused by weight and gravity, it is difficult to move. When the arms and club are "frozen" in one piece, and the torque to start them moving originates from one end of the system, it requires a brief but powerful move to set them into motion and complete the backswing <u>without</u> a lift from the hands and forearms, which we do **not** want to do. **Most amateurs trying to imitate Jack, start the swing too deliberately and cannot release the tension from the arms and wrists at the proper time, because the slow start creates a <u>need</u> to lift the arms and club in order to get them all the way back.** The lift leaves tension in the arms at the change of direction, which inhibits an effortless start to the delivery and subsequently throws the swing-plane off. We'll talk more about the change of direction momentarily.

THE CRITICAL FIRST RELEASE

The point where the tension leaves the arms is what I call the "first release" (photo A, page 76), and **its identification and definition may prove to be one of my most important contributions to golf.** The intensity of the heave, and a properly timed point of first release, are the major keys to maintaining timing and an ability to generate speed without effort. Incidentally, the first release is invisible both to the camera and the naked eye. **Inability to see the first release, and the subtlety of feeling it, has created most**

of the puzzle around swing mechanics for many, many years. Once you understand how the first release affects the rest of the swing, the entire picture of how the golf swing should work begins to take shape.

The reason that the first release is invisible, is as follows. When the body is standing upright, with the arms hanging relaxed, the arms do not hang at total possible extension. Natural elasticity within the muscles, causes the arms to hang about an inch or so above full extension. If you force the arms downward, and then allow them to relax, they will draw up slightly (about an inch). This you can see. However, in the golf swing, when the arms are forced to full extension just prior to starting the club back (you can see Jack Nicklaus do this very clearly), and then put into motion by the back and shoulders, the point where the tension leaves the arms (approximately seven-thirty) becomes invisible. Because of the centrifugal momentum imparted to the arms and club by the heave or first movement, the arms remain extended and do not draw up when the tension is released from them. The backswing continues beyond the seven-thirty point from the initial heave momentum alone, **and requires NO additional muscle power.** The heave, the first release, and the continuance of the backswing beyond the first release point, all appear smooth and deliberate even though **a total tension change in the arms and wrists has occurred at the seven-thirty point.** The arms, shoulders, and wrists, have **totally** relaxed and **SHOULD NOT RE-TIGHTEN through the change of direction or the remainder of the swing.** If tightening occurs during **ANY** part of the delivery, the speed of angular release between the club and arms coming into impact will be reduced and the efficiency of the swing diminished.

79

Understanding the first release and how it affects everything that happens subsequently in the swing, is a critical element in understanding the GRAVITY golf swing as a whole.

Photo B

THE WEIGHT TRANSFER

In a full swing, by the time the arms have reached the first release point, the left leg should have **completely** relaxed and the weight already begun to shift to the right side. At the point of first release, the left leg <u>could</u> fully leave the ground — as the transfer drill in the next chapter demonstrates. A **total** relaxation of the left leg **must** occur to allow proper weight transfer and to enable the body to correctly pivot against and around the right leg. Momentum from the heave should carry the body weight totally against a firm right leg, but **not** to a point where the right leg becomes vertical (that would be a sway). When the arms reach a point at approximately ten o'clock (photo B), they begin to stall or gently collapse. Up to this point, the arms and shoulders should remain comfortably extended due to centrifugal momentum, **NOT to forced extension.** When the arms begin to stall and the right elbow automatically starts to fold, the momentum from the heave (which has carried and held the body weight against the right leg) is released and **gravity** starts the weight transfer back to the left leg. The shoulders meanwhile, continue turning into the backswing as the weight falls back onto the left **heel,** and when the weight lands **fully** on that heel, they (the shoulders) are at maximum turn and the body is in a position called "full separation" or "coiled" (shoulders fully turned, weight back on left heel). By this time the right elbow has folded back into a tucked position and the forward body rotation of delivery is about to begin. Study the Normal Swing on page 122. Full separation is in photo 5.

BE CAREFUL OF THIS

It is very important that the arch muscle in the left foot be relaxed as the weight shifts back to the left leg, otherwise the body weight cannot fall easily back to the left heel and the delivery will not start properly. Correct rotary motion for the delivery requires a fixed left axis position. Because the foot attaches to the leg in an "L" shape, the pivotal axis (left leg) and the swing-plane will not remain in their proper positions if the delivery rotation is made from the toe portion (or "ball") of the left foot. **The entire axis leg will move backwards during delivery if the HEEL is not the pivot point.** If delivery is made by turning on the front of the foot, unless compensations are made (too spooky and unreliable), the shot will go off line. The considerable strength of the left foot arch must **NOT** be used for balance during the swing or it will cause problems with the swing flow and thus affect plane control. The arch muscles of the feet are **so powerful**, that unless the left arch is **completely** relaxed as the weight shifts back to the left leg, it will prevent the body weight from falling onto the heel. This will inhibit the next fundamental event from functioning properly. After the weight lands back on the left heel correctly, another

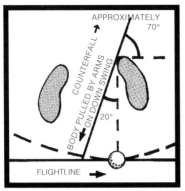

Fig. C   Counterfall Angle

CRITICAL (yet almost invisible) move must occur preceeding delivery, and the necessity for that movement must be explained.

THE ALL IMPORTANT COUNTERFALL

When a golf swing of **ANY** size is made, the downward movement of the arms, hands and club in the delivery prior to impact, creates a centrifugal force pulling against the body, toward and approximately twenty degrees to the player's right of the golf ball (see fig. C). If you will stand on your left foot only and swing the club to the top of the backswing, then start the delivery from a position of perfect balance, you can feel the body being pulled on the line that the diagram describes (be certain that you don't counterfall to offset those forces without realizing that you are doing so). Immediately upon starting down from a position of perfect balance, the swing-plane will move slightly to the outside, and an outside-in, or "over the top" delivery path will develop (not

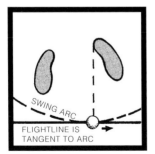

Fig. D   Tangent Release

good). The forces that pull against the body during delivery have occurred to some degree in **every** golf swing that ever has been (or will be) made.... the laws of physics say so. What this means to swing mechanics is as follows. **In order to maintain perfect balance during the golf swing, a**

82

force MUST be present to offset the pull from the swinging hands, arms and club against the body during delivery. This is achieved by initiating, **prior** to the downswing, a backwards fall (counterfall) **from** the left heel, on a line 180 degrees (dead opposite) from the forward pull of the hands, arms and club. When this is done properly, these counteracting forces are exactly equal and opposite — the body remains **off vertical** through impact, and perfect equilibrium is achieved throughout. The body returns to vertical as the follow-through is completed. Without the counterfall we would be pulled off balance in the down-swing and the swing-plane would leave its proper path. A correct counterfall causes the club path to move from inside the flightline to square at impact, and back to the inside on the follow through. The ball will be released on a line tangent to the arc, assuming that the clubface is perpendicular to the arc (square) at impact (fig. D).

The counterfall should begin on a vector approximately 70 degrees left of the intended flightline, or almost behind and over your left shoulder, and moves to the player's right as the club passes through the impact area (study fig. C carefully).

The counterfall is a **very** subtle movement, yet an **absolutely critical** one. Any time you witness someone coming badly "over the top" during delivery, you know that they are not making an adequate counterfall preceeding the downswing. The player will either pull, slice, or block the shot, or compensate for the plane change by clubface manipulation in order to hit the ball on line. The amount of counterfall required for each shot varies, depending on the speed of the delivery and the club selection. **The harder the swing, the greater the centrifugal pull from the hands, arms and club against the body, and the greater the counterfall needed to offset those forces.** If the correct degree of counterfall is utilized, exact equilibrium can be maintained through impact to the finish of the swing, and the golfer will wind up in perfect balance upon completion of the follow through. **Don't worry about having to calculate the proper degree of counterfall for each shot. When you train properly, you will teach yourself to do it automatically**. Most professionals aren't even aware that they counterfall preceeding delivery because of the subtlety of it. They know, if only subconsciously, that they will be off balance without it. You won't find mention of it in any of Jack's material and he does it as well as anyone who has ever played the game.

For totally efficient execution, **a proper counterfall is necessary in all forms of sports where pivotal motion occurs** in a throwing, slinging, or kicking movement. Examples would be pitching a baseball, a hammer throw, throwing a discus, a football, javelin, a tennis serve, a soccer style place kicker, etc.. Remember that during **every** golf swing you make, from 300 yard drives to two foot putts, the arms and club pull against the body in varying degrees. That pull against you **must be compensated for, otherwise the body cannot remain in perfect rotational equilibrium. If you ever tried to stand still over a little chip shot and then "chilly-dipped" or bladed the ball, you know what it means to swing with an improper or inadequate counterfall.** The next time some well intentioned person tells you that the key to a short shot is to stand still over it, close your ears. It is true that for a proper shot, the net result should be stability in the pivotal axis (left leg), or an appearance of standing still. **However, the hands and arms MUST MOVE to hit the shot, and THE PULL AGAINST THE BODY WHICH THAT MOVEMENT CREATES, MUST BE OFFSET in order to achieve stability in the axis (left leg) during delivery.** Because the overall mass is greater in the body, than in the arms, hands and club, which are doing the swinging, a very slight counterfall (an inch or two for a tee shot), will offset those forces. When the counterfall is executed properly, neither the pull from the club, arms and hands against the body during delivery — nor the counterfall — can easily be seen. They effectively negate each other, and the net result is an **APPEARANCE of stillness** created by perfect equilibrium in the pivoting axis. Remember that a ball hit even a half inch out of the center of the clubface, will result in a mis-hit shot. **The importance of a PRECISE degree of counterfall for every varying speed swing, cannot be overstated.** Don't forget, however, as I mentioned a moment ago, a **perfect** instinct for proper counterfall on every shot can be easily learned <u>without</u> having to think about it (next chapter).

MORE ABOUT WEIGHT TRANSFER

We need to digress for a moment and discuss weight transfer. This might be a good opportunity to check your overflow valve and grab a Darvon.... thanks for coming back. As you will see in the next chapter when you study the one-footed drills, it is not necessary to make any transfer of weight to hit a perfect golf shot. In fact, all shots of less than approximately 100 yards should be made from the left heel only and employ **no** transfer whatever, simply pivot back, **proper degree of counterfall** and pivot forward. The <u>only</u>

time we need to transfer weight, is when we are trying to hit a shot close to maximum distance. The use of weight transfer in the full swing, adds approximately five to ten percent additional club speed and equivalent percentage distance over a full swing that employs no transfer (as in the one-footed drills). A good rule to follow is that <u>unless you are making a full backswing, you do not want to make a weight shift.</u>

Follow me now: If you stand on your left foot only and pivot yourself into a counterfall, that counterfall will start **slowly**, as a tree begins to fall slowly when it is cut. The function of the weight transfer, when we want to hit the ball near maximum distance, is simply to add momentum to the start of the counterfall. This enables the pivotal movement of the delivery to begin <u>faster</u> **WITHOUT an output of energy from the arms and shoulders or right leg, which would put the swing in conflict with the third law of motion (action-reaction) and cause undesired swing-plane movement as well as an actual reduction in clubhead speed if the wrists tighten.** This is exactly why a pitcher has a mound from which to pitch. The fall from the mound onto the front leg, creates greater momentum, a faster starting counterfall, and greater subsequent pivotal speed without increased effort. This allows the pitcher to whip his "rag-like" arm harder than he could from the flat ground, <u>without</u> throwing off his control.

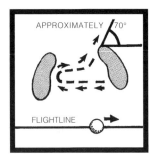

Fig. E Weight Deflection

In the golf swing, when the weight shifts to the right leg and then falls back to the left leg, it (the

weight) is moving laterally. When the weight lands back on the left leg, there should be just enough resistance from the left leg **to deflect the lateral movement into the counterfall** (see fig. E), which again, begins on a vector approximately 70 degrees left of the intended flightline. The weight transfer back to the left leg must be complete by the time the shoulders reach the completion of their backturn.

It is very important that on any shot where a weight transfer is employed, the transfer be 100%. A 100% transfer is defined as **approximately the farthest distance one can fall from the right foot to the left foot, and still clear the hip turn level.** If the feet are too far apart in the stance, the body will fall too much against the left leg in the second half of the transfer, and an upward level change in the hips will be necessary to complete the follow through. It requires an output of energy from either the right leg, or the shoulders and arms, to clear the turn from a "jammed" position. Swing efficiency is lessened and the integrity of the swing-plane is difficult to maintain when this happens. If the feet are placed too close together at address, there is inadequate momentum in the fall from the right foot to the left foot to start the counterfall with enough speed to achieve the desired rotational speed for the delivery. If that didn't immediately sink in, read it until it does. The reason for the importance of not having the feet too close together is this. If the brain senses an inadequate degree of fall momentum in the transfer, it will **involuntarily** trigger a flexing action in the body to achieve the desired and anticipated swing speed. Again the swing-plane is violated, and the player falls victim to the third law of motion. **As a general rule, whenever the brain senses an inadequacy of any kind in the golf swing, it will attempt,**

INVOLUNTARILY, to make up for it with some type of APPLIED force. Bad News! In order to achieve total efficiency and effortlessness in the swing, it is imperative that involuntary backlashes are avoided by correct set-up and proper movement from the very beginning of the swing.

Delivery of the arms, club and body through the impact area should be all **rotary** on the left leg or pivotal axis. There should be **no** lateral movement during delivery. **All the lateral movement of the weight transfer, both to the right foot and back to the left, occurs during the takeaway.** The movement of delivery is analogous to closing a fixed hinge door, except that the top of the pivotal axis (the left shoulder) is <u>not fixed</u> (as the heel is to the ground), and therefore requires a counterfall to keep the delivery from pulling the entire pivotal axis (left heel to left shoulder) out of position. Most golfers have some degree of backward movement (away from target) in the left hip or pivotal axis due to applied force from the upper body and the resultant leverage that goes back against the axis. When this problem occurs during the downswing, it causes the body to move somewhat like a revolving door instead of a fixed hinge door. This allows some of the power to escape as the left hip moves backwards, as well as causing the swing-plane to shift to the left or "over the top." If a player's weight ends up on the right foot in the follow through, it is evidence of <u>applied</u> force(s) or improper counterfall during the delivery.

THE CHANGE OF DIRECTION

Let's go back for a moment and talk about the change of direction since it is another critical part of the swing. **It is very important that the origin (proper muscles) and intensity of the heave, which starts the backswing, be precisely correct; so that when coupled with a proper first release point, the arms and club will begin to stall exactly when they should.** As previously mentioned, the desired amount of shoulder turn required to initiate the counterfall should be attainable without **ANY** lift from the hands and arms. **It should be accomplished with heave momentum alone.** When the arms reach the stall point (between ten and eleven o'clock in a full swing), the folding of the right arm as it collapses, should cantelever the club through twelve o'clock. From the twelve o'clock position, the club and arms should "free fall" into the beginning of the delivery as the shoulders continue turning back. By the time the club has fallen to between two and three o'clock, the shoulders have completed their turn, the right arm has fallen into a "tucked" position, the counterfall has occurred, and the forward rotation of the body on the left heel automatically begins and starts pulling the arms and club into the delivery (page 122, photo 6). As centrifugal force begins to develop and increase during the downswing (assuming the wrists are **tension free**), it will effectively create the angular release (second release) of the wrists into impact, and the shoulders, arms and club will be at full extension when the ball is struck. **If the momentum of the heave and the first release point are correct, the change of direction will occur BY ITSELF, with absolutely ZERO necessity to tighten the shoulders, arms or wrists.** As a result of a perfectly timed change of direction, the shoulders, arms and wrists may remain **tension free** throughout the delivery. The swing will work like a backwards whip, with the <u>arms</u> representing the <u>soft end</u> of the whip and the club representing the handle.

Why is it so important to have relaxed arms during the change of direction? For several reasons: One, the body is at its <u>most vulnerable</u> position from a standpoint of balance, when the arms are up and going through the change of direction. When the arms are changing directions, **any** tension increases **whatsoever** from the shoulders, arms and hands, send <u>some</u> degree of energy and leverage back against the body, which subsequently works to throw off the balance and the positional integrity of the swing-plane (causes mis-hit shots). **The downward starting movement should begin by the forces of GRAVITY ALONE.**

Photo F

Another reason that the shoulders and arms should remain relaxed as the direction change occurs and delivery begins, is because of the body's lack of pivotal strength. The body has <u>very limited power</u> from a rotational standpoint because most of the lower body muscles run longitudinally. If you stand side by side someone, facing opposite directions, and hook arms, it is very easy to stop even a powerful individual from pivoting (see photo F). In the golf swing, arm and shoulder tension during the change of direction and downswing, has a similar effect against pivotal ability — as if you were to swing to the top of the backswing, grab a tree limb, and try to pivot forward. The degree of resistance won't be as severe as that example, **but a tension increase in the arms can EASILY create enough pivotal resistance to throw off the balance and swing-plane** thereby affecting ball contact and control. It also reduces speed and distance.

This raises another important point. Club speed is greatly affected by the degree of tension in the wrists at the point of angular (or second) release into and through impact. The speed at which the angles between the forearms and clubshaft are released is a measure of overall club-speed. **If the delivery is begun with an increase in tension in the shoulders, arms, wrists and hands, resistance to the angular release of the wrists coming into impact occurs.** In other words, the harder you try to hit the ball with tension, the more you slow the club down. It's sort of like pouring wet concrete, instead of oil, into the wrists while you are coming into impact. Although a flexing movement in the parts of the upper body will indeed bring the club down (Arnold Palmer), it simultaneously causes a <u>reduction</u> in release speed by creating tension in the wrists, which fights to inhibit the angular release. Because of his incredible strength, Arnold could literally "rake" or beat the ball with his shoulders and arms and

91

hit it a long way. With better mechanics he might have easily outdriven Jack on a consistent basis, but because of technical imperfections it was difficult for him to do so (I still love him). Arnold didn't block that hook for nothing! He was terrified of it, although it stretches my imagination to envision Arnold being afraid of anything. However, I can speak with authority on the frightening aspects of a pull hook. Maybe he wasn't as spooked as I was because he was strong enough to usually block it out. I wasn't. Arnold probably just viewed the hook as a malady of existence, and the "block" as something to give his swing individualism. Nevertheless, it is much easier to create club speed with relaxed wrists and rotary torque from the left leg and hip. The more the wrists are relaxed on the downswing, the easier it is for the turn to whip the club into impact with acceleration. Also, back-pressure is not exerted against the body and the swing-plane, and control is not a problem.

THE WRIST COCK AND DELIVERY

The cocking of the wrists in the swing should occur **naturally** as a result of heave momentum from the back and shoulders and the release of tension at the first release point. The cocking of the wrists should begin very subtly and continue throughout the takeaway and the change of direction. After the swing is started in one piece and the first release occurs at about seven-thirty, the momentum of the club (since it is lighter) will cause the club to start gaining on the heavier arms and cocking the now relaxed wrists. It is very important in the full swing that the wrists cock **subtly** throughout the change of direction and do **NOT** finish cocking until it is time for them to release into impact (see photo 6, page 122). **One of the most deadly sins in golf is to start the wrists cocking by lifting the club with the hands instead of allowing the momentum of the heave to cock them for you.** Doing this can cause the club to gain too quickly on the arms in the takeaway, ultimately causing an involuntary tension increase in the wrists in order to stop or slow the club down for the change of direction (trouble starts). This tension causes a **reduction** in delivery speed, as well as energy being turned back against the body and the swing-plane, causing plane movement. If the wrists are cocked as a result of the **proper** amount of heave momentum at the beginning of the takeaway, with tension free wrists from the first release point on, **there will NOT be a need to hold a set or cocked position in the wrists during the downswing.** This is because the wrists will not finish cocking until it is time for them to "let go" at the second or angular release point. If the wrists are <u>too</u> cocked at the change of direction, there is a tendency for the forward turn of the body to cause a "pitch-out" or early release coming into delivery and the hands will be behind the clubhead at impact (not good). Proper timing, created by correct origin of takeaway, proper heave momentum and first release, will allow total wrist freedom from the point of first release throughout the remainder of the swing. **NO manipulation to keep the arms and club "in plane" should be necessary** and maximum release speed into and through impact will occur.

Once the counterfall has begun and the arms have "free fallen" to the point where the wrists are ready to release into impact, muscular torsion from the gluteal muscles of the pivotal leg (left) can be blended **smoothly** into the rotational move to create maximum acceleration through impact. This should be the **only** muscular source of power within the swing and comes from **within** the axis and **not from an extraneous source** (arms, shoulders, or right leg). The hips should <u>never</u> be "thrown" through the ball, but simply blended into the turn with torque from the hip, which will <u>not</u> disrupt the balance.

As previously mentioned, impact in a correct golf swing should be **totally incidental** with no intent to strike or flex in the delivery. The follow through will occur naturally, assuming that nothing is done to restrict it. Balance at the finish of the swing is a <u>result</u> of everything having been done properly in the beginning. In the follow through, the right leg works like a <u>boat anchor</u> to keep the momentum of the swing from pulling the body off balance. The inside toe edge of the right shoe sole drags <u>after</u> impact and slows down the follow through momentum.

WE DID IT!

This fairly well concludes the most essential mechanics and how they work. There are a number of things I have omitted, but they are of secondary importance and will be covered later. If the explanation already seems overly complicated, don't be concerned. **A correct and totally efficient golf swing is <u>indeed</u> a very <u>complex</u> mechanism.** If it weren't, so many bright and determined people would not handle their clubs as poorly as they do — nor would there be such an atmosphere of mystery surrounding the game. As I have mentioned, it is **not** necessary to either understand or consciously think about all these things in order to instill and perfectly coordinate them in your body. If I have failed to communicate a clear picture of how all the parts and mechanics relate, some <u>proper</u> practice will certainly do that for you. Many of my students have told me that something they read several times in one of my articles finally became clear to them once they "felt" it. We have been discussing a number of things which are <u>extremely</u> subtle in nature. Fortunately, they can all be learned to perfection with very little <u>conscious</u> thought. As previously stated, however, the advantage that you will gain from understanding tension relationships and mechanics, will enable you to be totally self-taught. Once the picture of how everything works is completely clear in your mind, it will always be easy for you to find the <u>root</u> cause if something is going wrong. Forgive my redundancy, but this is a <u>very</u> important point. **Working on the wrong part of the swing can create a series of compensating moves that make the action so complex, as well as putting it in conflict with physics laws, that ultimate development and reliability under pressure are <u>next to impossible.</u>**

If I have convinced you that this is indeed how a "perfect" golf swing does and should function, open your mind a little further and read the next chapter. I'll show you how to teach yourself to swing just as well as the great Gravity players...... and that it can be done so easily and relatively quickly, as to amaze even the most hardline skeptics. Trust me, **this works.** You learned how to walk perfectly and efficiently, didn't you? How much did you know about ambulatory physics back then? **Think about it!** There is a fabulous computer available in your head **if** you know the access code.

Chapter Six

Training the Swing

THE EASY WAY IS BEST

One of the oddities that makes life interesting is that there is a hard way and an easy way to do most anything. More often than not, the easy way is also the correct way. Usually, the hard part is knowing what the easy way is.

Beginning this "most fun" chapter reminds me of a great story. When I first started in the golf business in 1965, I was working as an assistant pro at Knollwood Golf Club, in Granada Hills, California. One of the closest friendships that I developed there was with an airline pilot named Roy Watts. Whether or not Roy is still alive I do not know, but even if he's not, I'm sure he's well preserved. We consumed enough fruit and grain by-products in those two years to have pickled half the cucumbers in the San Fernando Valley. Man!.... Am I glad my head doesn't feel like that in the morning nowadays. Notwithstanding the hangovers, we did, however, share a lot of memorable times.

Roy was full of good yarns, and he swore this one was true. As the story goes, Roy was in the control tower at L.A. International one overcast day, when an F-104 fighter pilot from Mississippi made an emergency landing for fuel. After the guy gasses up, he's back out on the taxiway waiting to leave, and Roy is listening to the flight controller giving him instructions for the take-off. The instructions were extremely complex, with a number of vector changes and orders to hold on each vector and altitude for so many seconds, until he had cleared the traffic pattern. According to Roy, it took the controller about five minutes just to go through the data. When he had finished, the pilot calls back on the radio in his Mississippi drawl..... "Uhhh.... saaay goood buuddy, woouuld yoouu miind reepeeeatin thaaat.... pleeease?" Naturally, everyone in the control tower cracks up. After the laughter subsides, the controller begins again to go through the take-off instructions. When he's about half finished, the pilot interrupts..... "saaay maaan, I'm sittin out heere wiith a mach 3 aiirplaane and a mach 1 braain.... how aboouut cleearin mee straaight uup?" When everyone is through rolling on the floor, the controller concedes straight-up clearance. The F-104 comes haulin' down the runway, the pilot turns the nose up, hits the after-burner and is gone in a flash of fire! About thirty seconds later, he comes back on the radio.... "Hi!.... it's mee agin! Awwn top at fortee thoouusand feeet aand awwl is cleeear.... **bye!**"

There's a common thread in that story pertaining to one of the main objectives of this book, which is to demonstrate that the entire approach to learning the proper way to swing a golf club has been too complicated for hundreds of years. **In fact, it has been totally backwards.** That's a big mouthful, but unfortunately for most folks, it's true. For certain, the game has not been taught in a manner which prompts the player to achieve totally efficient mechanics, nor in a way that encourages the most rapid development. Most golfers learn by trial and error over a period of many years, and tend to pick up a number of compensating measures for technical mistakes along the way. It should not be too difficult to elicit agreement that, **ideally,** one would prefer to learn **correctly** (in compliance with good physics practices) so that ultimate development would not be impaired and that maximum reliability under pressure could be attained.

WHY DRILLS?

To train the swing to its highest potential level of development, employing the most physics compliant mechanics, we use several uniquely designed drills. Remember that in the previous chapter we discussed the fact that a "perfect" swing has very little feeling since the efficiency of movements are at such a peak. Trying to verbally communicate all the proper movements while the student is in a normal swing mode of full strength and maximum balance (both hands on the club and the feet spread apart), is next to impossible. Even when it can be accomplished through conventional approach, it normally requires many years of practice, trial and error. **The finished (normal) swing mode is the most technically subtle way you can swing because strength and balance have an ability to partially cover up mechanical flaws. One of the main functions of the drills is to magnify errors so that any technical mistakes are easy for the player to feel.** We arrive at the "nothing" feeling of a perfect swing through a "back door" approach. By eliminating things that obviously feel wrong in the drills, and simply searching for the technique which will give desired results to the drills (which are not that hard to find) we acquire the "nothing" feeling. As mentioned throughout this book, **the drills are designed to *isolate correct mechanics within the player* whether <u>or not</u> he/she knows exactly what those mechanics might be.**

BACKWARDS FOR 500 YEARS

Before explaining how to do the drills, let's take a look at how the game has been taught backwards since its inception. **Note** that I did **not** say it was played backwards, only that it was taught that way. When an individual learns to swing a golf club through traditional methods, he utilizes an **expanded safety envelope**. "Whoa!.... is that anything like a parachute?" Well, yes and no. If you will stand up straight, place your feet together (touching), now **without bending at the waist or moving either foot,** draw a circle with your body like a tree swaying in the breeze. Go as far as you can in every direction without moving the feet or bending. The circle is not very large, but there's enough latitude in it that there is no danger from falling when we stay in the center of it, and as long as we're sober and the legs enjoy available mobility. That circle is called your "safety envelope" (fig. A). Your brain will do **everything** in its power to keep you from violating the edge of your safety envelope, **including teaching you to swing a golf club exactly like Jack Nicklaus.** I'm not puttin' you on!

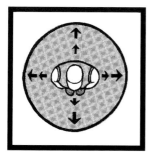

Fig. A Safety Envelope

The way that golf has traditionally been taught is with the feet spread apart, which expands or broadens the safety envelope. When the envelope is expanded, thereby giving the body's balance extra security or margin for error, **every conceivable INCORRECT instinct that could surface in a**

golfer's mind.... usually does. Normal instinct from a spread-footed stance is to utilize some degree of upper body <u>force</u> in the swing. You can witness this instinct even in small children when they first pick up a golf club. Every one of the little beggars — including my own — wants to beat the "dogmeat" out of the ball. Remember that when the arms <u>tighten</u> during delivery, <u>in addition</u> to bringing the club down, they work like two "pump handles" — back against the pivotal axis, tending to throw the body off balance. Follow this **carefully**. When the feet are spread and the safety envelope expanded, it is possible to apply enough force from the arms and shoulders during delivery, to create ample back-pressure against the body — and subsequent movement in the swing-plane — to cause the player to "whiff" the ball — **without creating sufficient back-pressure against the system to cause a violation of the edge of the envelope, thus threatening the body through falling.** Frequently you'll see a player completely miss the ball, but it's rare to see someone swing the club and fall down, unless they slip. **As long as the edge of the envelope is not threatened, the portions of the brain that maintain balance and equilibrium (cerebellum and vestibular system) don't really <u>care</u> what type of swing mechanics are employed. If the swing procedure doesn't imperil the body, through falling or otherwise, the brain will allow you to proceed in WHATEVER fashion you consciously think is right.** If your concept of hitting a golf ball is "lift and chop," your sub-conscious will allow you to swing that way <u>throughout your life</u>, as long as it does **not** detect a <u>potential threat</u> to your well-being. Besides, if your brain doesn't know how it feels to swing the club <u>exactly</u> like Jack, then how can it know what it's missing?

Remember, **your conscious mind** (cerebral cortex) **wants to hit the ball.** A <u>totally</u> correct and efficient golf swing requires an **enormous** number of perfectly coordinated movements and proper tension relationships between the body's parts. If we leave the cerebellum on "cruise control," so to speak, with a large safety envelope surrounding the body (feet spread), it will "sit back and relax," while the cerebral cortex (conscious-mind) attempts to train the golf swing <u>one excruciating step</u> at a time. **When a broad safety envelope is employed during the learning process, many deviant and incorrect procedures can be employed by the "not so smart" conscious mind — and a golf swing which is a physics "nightmare" can easily develop.** When the brain feels the security of balance of the spread-footed stance, the typical plan in the conscious mind is to use **excessive upper body force.**

YOUR SUBCONSCIOUS IS AMAZING

The developmental process for a decent swing, under conventional teaching techniques, normally takes years. Personally, that's far too slow to suit me. The brain, however, is capable of programming countless simultaneous functions within the system relatively quickly, and has an innate capacity for instilling the most efficient movements possible into the body. Just as it taught us to walk in a totally efficient manner as children, it can teach us to swing a golf club with the same degree of perfection. **The trick is in knowing how to access the appropriate parts of the brain and get them to take charge of your training.**

The following sentence is one of the most important ones in this book. **If we can create and employ a practice technique, whereby ANY incorrect mechanical movements, which would ultimately cause swing-plane movement and mis-hit shots, will ALSO cause a potential threat to the body through falling, the circuits responsible for maintaining balance will "wake up" and force us to stop making those improper movements.** We establish this situation through a unique set of one-footed drills which "**shrink** the safety envelope." As I am about to explain, by teaching the swing from a "shrunken safety envelope," instead of an expanded one, we can **force** the sub-conscious or lower cortex to program **totally efficient mechanics** within the system in order to protect itself. **By making the safety envelope smaller, and learning to function within the confines of it, we can develop greater equilibrium and swing-plane control and enjoy more properly struck shots as BY-PRODUCTS of developing better balance.** Again, if we train with a small enough envelope, any incorrect movements which would cause mis-hit shots, will now **also** cause a threat to the balance. Before the brain will allow you to literally throw yourself on the ground, **it will teach you to swing in a totally efficient manner.** What we are doing, is just like learning to walk all over again, only this time we are going to have **one less leg** and be swinging the club at the same time. Don't panic, the marvelous cerebellum can handle the task quite easily!

The drills we use are so demanding by design, that **they will isolate Jack's golf swing,** in its perfect form, **in YOUR body**, without you even knowing what is happening. They do this because the parameters of the drills are so stringent that only Jack's style of swing, the GRAVITY swing, is high enough in technical merit to give positive results during the drills. None of the other swing styles employ good enough physics to achieve the same level of ball flight excellence in the exercises. Having a way to isolate perfect mechanics in the body through sub-conscious programming is exciting! **Using these special drills to manipulate the hierarchy within the brain represents an entirely new approach to learning, which is not limited to golf.** Any sport where extraneous leverage and tension create a potential threat to the body's balance, can be taught more effectively using these techniques. **I'm also one hundred percent convinced that these drills may enable many athletes, including baseball pitchers, to avoid rotator cuff and various other injuries caused by improper mechanics.** Your golf swing will also become less of a strain on your body, **especially your lower back**, as your mechanics improve.

Over the past eighteen years, I've developed about fifty different drills in an attempt to isolate perfect mechanics within various individuals. What I've observed is that although each of these drills can impart beneficial qualities to the swing, the majority of them can be "faked" to some degree. In other words, some level of positive results can be achieved without "isolating" totally efficient movement within the system. This leaves us short of the goal of developing a swing that's at its highest mechanical, and therefore potentially reliable, level. Remember that, **ideally, we are trying to develop a swing that generates maximum club-speed, for minimum energy input.** The more efficient the swing becomes, the less likelihood there is that the balance and swing-plane will be thrown off (affecting control) in the process of achieving distance. The fifty or so drills have been continually refined to the point that we now use only about four basic drills, with some variations.

The best of the drills (and the ones which will isolate the most correct technique within the body the fastest) are the one-footed drills. You may have seen golfers hitting balls standing on one foot before, but we do it quite a bit differently.

A WORD OF CAUTION

Before I explain the procedures for doing the drills, a few words of caution are in order. **The one-footed drills are physically demanding and should be undertaken with the same precautionary and sensible procedures of any other exercise program.** Work into them gradually, starting with only a few golf balls for each drill. Do only the number of drills to begin with that you can handle fairly comfortably. You will probably fatigue quickly at first, depending on your physical condition and the quality of your mechanics. As your pivotal axis (left leg) strengthens, your ability to prolong the drill with more golf balls, will increase. Remember, the drills are designed to isolate <u>total</u> efficiency of movement and <u>perfect</u> mechanics in your body. If in the beginning, you are having a difficult time achieving positive results with the drills, it does **not** by any means indicate that you're uncoordinated, that you're a bad person, or that you can't go play golf and have fun! It simply means that there are still mechanical imperfections in your swing and that room for improvement exists. It won't help anything to get mad at yourself if you're not hitting the ball perfectly from the drills.

In fact, it will <u>increase</u> your level of tension and make the drills even **more** difficult to do. Use the drills the way they are designed—as training tools and study guides for you to know whether or not you're on the right track. As your swing efficiency increases, the drills will become easier to do, and when you can do them perfectly, you'll be fully trained. **Your normal swing will be trained completely from the drills without even working in the "finished product" mode.**

THE ONE-FOOTED DRILLS

Begin the one-footed drills by lining up a row of about five golf balls, perpendicular to the target, about four or five inches apart (page 124, fig. 1). Take a five or six iron to try the drill for the first time. Back away from the line of balls about six or eight feet. Now, pretend that where your right leg used to be.... you get the picture.... there is nothing. Pick your right foot <u>completely off</u> the ground about an inch or two. Do **not** bend your right knee too much and lift the foot back behind you, because doing so will move your balance toward the ball of your left foot, which we don't want. You are now going to **hop** over to the line of balls (should take at least three hops), take your grip with both hands, and begin hitting full shots. **The little trip over to the line of balls is important because it shrinks your safety envelope and makes you very sensitive to balance**. You may hit the balls as hard as you wish. Hit as many as you can comfortably tolerate and then hop back to the point where you started. **During the entire time you are hopping up to the line of balls, hitting them, and hopping back to the starting point, your right foot should <u>never</u> touch the ground (don't use the club as a crutch either)**. Stop a second! If you are getting older and are ready to heave the book at the fireplace after reading that last sentence, just hang on a minute. We have excellent drills tailored for all ages and body strengths. It is not my intent to maim or torture anybody. Many of my students are up in their sixties and seventies and can do many of the drills, including the one-footers, with ease and agility. The important thing is, if you can handle the physical demands of the one-footed drills, they will teach you faster than any other technique. If you are not strong enough to do them at first, don't worry. There are other drills you can do to vastly improve your timing and the quality of your mechanics. You can quickly improve your leg strength to the point where you should be able to do the one-footed drills, by putting on your sneakers and spending a few minutes each day hopping around the privacy of your home on either foot alone (especially the left foot if you are a right handed player).

The golf ball can be hit from one leg only, more than ninety percent of the distance it can be hit with both feet on the ground. To your amazement, as soon as you become accustomed to the drills, you'll probably hit the ball farther, more solidly and straighter standing on one leg than on two. Your one-footed swing will quickly become better than your two-footed swing out of necessity to maintain balance. Once the higher quality of your one-footed swing works its way into your two-footed swing, **which it WILL do,** you will then hit the ball farther from two feet.

When you hop up and address the first ball, your left foot should be turned about 30 degrees open or to your left. You must start the swing correctly, as described in the last chapter, or you will lose your balance. **Try as hard as you can**

106

not to touch the right foot to the ground during the entire drill (as many swings as you can comfortably tolerate). Assuming that you have no problems with your internal balance mechanisms, if you have trouble with your balance while you are hopping up to the ball or at address, it is an indicator that you are too tense or that your legs are out of condition. If the swing is executed properly, the follow through will pull you off the left leg (since your right foot is not on the ground to anchor you) and you will hop, after each shot, **from your left foot, to your left foot,** at about a forty-five degree angle to the left of your flight-line and forward. (see fig. 7 & 8, page 125) You will make about two hops of a foot or so in length, on that line. Then, without touching the right foot to the ground, you must **hop** back to the next ball and swing again. Once all the balls have been hit (or as many as you feel comfortable with.... at least two), **hop** back to your starting point.

Now listen-up! None of these drills are designed to amuse me or to make anyone look foolish. They have been developed through years of study, trial and error, to instill precise mechanical movements into anyone who does them, and that is EXACTLY what they do. If you will practice these drills, you will very quickly begin to swing the club in a more efficient manner, and before long, you'll start to "feel in yourself" what you see in Jack Nicklaus.

To derive full benefit from the one-footed drills, it is very important not to "cheat" when you are doing them. Here's how they miraculously work if you will do them correctly. If you hop up to the line of balls and make an improper swing, you will throw yourself off balance (not

107

down, just off balance). It is <u>very</u> important **not** to put your right foot down to save yourself from falling. You must save yourself with your **left** leg only (remember not to use the club as a crutch). **Putting your right foot down to save yourself after an improper swing, lets your brain "off the hook" for any need to re-program your incorrect movements because the potential threat of falling is gone.** If you make a poor swing in the drill, and put your right foot down to save your balance, the lazy part in your brain says.... "thanks for putting that foot down, it's easier for you to thrash at the ball and put that foot down to save yourself from crashing to the ground, than it is for me to teach you how to swing like Jack." In that case, it allows you to continue with your improper swing. On the other hand, if you make a poor swing, lose your balance, and are fighting to maintain balance on your left leg, **something quite different and amazing happens.** Your cerebellum, **sensing the struggle and the potential threat of falling,** comes off of "cruise control," where it has been with the expanded envelope, and says.... "hey!.... where is your other leg?" Since you are determined that you're **not** going to use the right leg to save yourself, your response is.... "it's gone, I don't have it anymore." **Your cerebellum is <u>forced</u> to accept the fact that you are now a one-legged person and senses its responsibility.** It says.... "well.... if you're determined to go through life swinging that stick over and over again, on only one leg, **you can't keep doing it like that.** The inefficiency of your movements is going to make you quickly fatigue and eventually **fall**. I (cerebellum still talking) need to teach you how to move with equilibrium and proper motion so that you can stay up on that leg as long as possible <u>without going down</u>." **AND IT <u>WILL</u> DO IT!**

WE'VE LEARNED THIS ALREADY

A similar process was probably at work when we learned to walk, only this time you're learning to walk on one leg while swinging a golf club at the same time. When a baby first stands upright, he/she is very unstable. The muscle tone and coordination have not developed to the point where there is efficiency of movement. If a child was placed in non-conventional social and cultural surroundings where it could not observe others walking upright, it might not choose to stand up at all because there is greater security (balance) in crawling on all fours. My wife swears "she didn't descend from no monkey," but it is my opinion that a youngster's main inspiration for standing up is that he sees people around him walking and wishes to do likewise. As the infant learns to stand and balance himself on two feet, gradually the balance and equilibrium circuits in the brain adapt to the new position of the head in space and the toddler soon begins to take those first few unassisted steps. Since man is built to function as an upright individual, it is part of the brains responsibility to teach him to walk in this gravity-threatened position (upright) with energy efficient motion. Imagine an adult walking like a toddler. He'd either be exhausted by ten o'clock in the morning, or he'd be much stronger. **Inasmuch as the margins of latitude and error have been reduced by shrinking the safety envelope, the one-footed drills are extremely fatiguing if the swing is not mechanically correct. The cerebellum and vestibular system sense this imbalance and quickly set about to coordinate the activity of ALL the moving body parts in order to achieve the goal of biomechanically efficient movement.** As mentioned earlier, perfect control of the swing-plane, and "dead-solid" shots come as **by-products** of developing the ability to function efficiently within the shrunken safety envelope.

ONE-ARMED DRILLS

To further isolate proper mechanics in the swing, we can weaken the body along with shrinking the safety envelope. The most demanding forms of the one-footed drills are when using either arm alone. All we need to hit a golf ball "dead flush" and straight, is one pivotal axis (left leg), one connection to the club (either arm), and proper movement in the swing. The one-armed, one-footed drills, are the most difficult of all the drills to "fake" (get results without totally correct mechanics), and consequently are the **most isolating** to proper procedure of any I have yet devised. If you cannot do them with desired results, it means there is still room for improvement in your swing. They are done exactly as the two-armed, one-footed drills, only with **no** aid from the opposite arm.

When doing the one-armed, one-footed drills, you should attempt to swing as hard as possible while maintaining full directional control over the ball. We are trying to learn to generate maximum speed without sacrificing accuracy, which makes it important to go "flat out" in the drills. If you practice just "meeting" the ball in the drills, without learning how to generate speed, the drills will not fully train your normal swing. You must allow the drills to teach you how to generate speed through **counterfall, rotational torque, timing and relaxed arms,** instead of through tension and applied force.

WATCH YOUR GRAB POINT

Everyone has in their golf swing, be it a right-armed, left-armed, or two-armed swing, what I call a "grab point." That's a point where the centrifugal force of the turn causes the arms to rise like the blades of a helicopter as they pick up speed. When the brain senses that the rising of the arms and club will cause the clubhead to miss the ball, it will make either or both arms tighten to try and hold the club in the swing-track. If this occurs, the club slows down and the swing-plane moves (mis-hits). The longer you allow the arms and club to fall (up to a point) before applying torque from the pivotal hip in the turn, the more speed you can generate without the clubhead missing the ball. It's simply a function of timing, which you will learn by doing one-armed swings. It's important to identify and isolate your "grab point" and know exactly how much speed you can generate without triggering it. As you get stronger through practicing, and as your timing improves, you will extend your grab point to greater and greater club speed. When one goes into a normal swing mode to play, if he knows at what speed his grab point will occur, the smart player will back down a notch and **not** flirt with it. Bad things generally happen when you do — like visiting the peripheral areas of the golf course.

When you first begin doing the one-armed, one-footed drills, you may notice that one arm is weaker than the other (usually the left). Try to apportion your practice time so that the weaker arm catches up to the other arm in its ability to control the club. You can have one perfectly trained arm and still not achieve desired results in a two-armed normal swing because the improperly functioning arm will pull the good one out of the swing-plane during delivery. We <u>ideally</u> want <u>two</u> **perfectly** trained arms, working together. Trying to rely on two 50% functioning arms to make a 100% swing, is not nearly as desirable or reliable as having two 100% trained arms making up a 200% swing. That margin for error comes in handy when the "heat" goes up.

After your leg becomes fatigued from doing one-footed drills, be they either right-armed, left-armed, (pages 132-133) or both-armed, you may then practice from a normal stance using either arm alone or you may practice the "no reference" or "transfer" drills which I am about to explain. If you are doing full swing right-arm drills, either from one foot or both feet, start the takeaway from a forward position (photo B). Starting right-handers from a normal position behind the ball creates a tendency to pick the club up (bad). It is much easier to heave the club into motion with the back, as it should be, from the forward position. Left handers may be started from behind the ball as in a normal swing.

Photo B

To hit solid, properly tracking (at the target) shots from a one-handed mode requires proper origin in the takeaway (back and both shoulders), perfect intensity of starting speed, and a perfectly timed first release (tension release) point.

112

Practicing with either arm alone is **NOT** teaching you to <u>hit</u> the ball with that arm. It is doing <u>exactly the opposite</u>. You are being taught to swing using proper physical mechanics. If you attempt to "strike" the ball with the strength of either arm, you will be unlikely to make contact and will definitely not enjoy maximum club speed and control. When you swing one-handers correctly, you are teaching yourself to make contact with timing, and speed generation through counterfall, proper forward pivot and centrifugal force.

The one-legged drills teach the fundamental timing mechanisms for the entire swing, including full swing, short game and putter. Once you become adept at them, and at one-legged, one-armed drills, you can employ two-armed and one-arm no reference and transfer drills to complete the training of your full swing. As mentioned in chapter five, the proper use of weight transfer will bring your swing up to full speed potential.

NO REFERENCE DRILLS

Of all the drills that I've developed which are designed to be done on two feet, the "no reference" drills are by far the best and have a dramatic effect on everyone who does them. They are fantastic for anyone who cannot stand the physical demands of the one-footed drills. The "no reference" drills may be done with both hands on the club or with either arm alone (pages 126-127, 130-131). To really isolate proper movement in the swing, they may, if one desires, be done in a one-footed mode as well. Here's how they work and why they are so effective.

Within the body and extremities are tiny sensors called proprioceptors which the brain uses to locate our parts in space. For example: If I want to move my hand and arm to a certain location either in front of or to any other relative position to my body, my brain isolates the position by way of the proprioceptors. The arm moves on a set of three dimensional or x, y, z coordinates. The arm may appear to be sitting motionless once a desired spot has been located, yet it will still be making minute movements in order to keep that position pin-pointed. The brain makes a memory record of the location and for a short time we can return the arm, if moved, back to almost that same position. This whole process is called proprioception.

Under the conventional approach to learning golf, we utilize the proprioceptive system in our arms to the detriment of developing proper swing mechanics. When we set the clubhead behind the ball at address, the brain locates the ball partially (visually also) <u>via</u> the proprioceptors in the arms. We then swing the club back, change directions and start the club down using the memory of where the arms were at address as a spot to which to return. When the arms "hunt" the ball in the downswing, both they and the club work as levers <u>against</u> the body and we get an effect like that of the "tail wagging the dog." Balance and swing-plane control <u>can be</u> easily compromised when this occurs.

Ideally, we should address the ball with a "mobile" posture, move the body in a dynamic fashion in the swing, with the arms being delivered **totally** by gravity and body rotation, with the ball being <u>incidentally</u> in the path of the clubhead. No "hunting" the ball with the arms should be done. This drill will inform you very quickly whether or not you are dependent on your arms to hit the ball.

To do the drill, set up as many balls in a line as you wish (pages 126-127). Back off about six feet away from the balls, take your grip, then hold the club vertically with the clubhead pointed up. The arms should be relaxed, elbows folded and the hands even with your breastbone. Then walk over and take your address to the first ball using your vision **only**, still keeping the club pointed up (fig. 1). Do **NOT** get the clubhead **anywhere near** the ball as you take your stance and set-up. If you do, the brain has located the ball with the arms and the value of the drill will be lost.

Once you "feel" that the ball is in the proper position relative to the body, push the club straight up until the hands are about even or slightly higher than the top of your head. The shoulder joints should feel extended (no slack). Still keeping the club pointed vertically, turn your shoulders a full 90 degrees back, allowing your weight to shift to the right foot and back to the left foot by the time they (shoulders) have completed the 90 degree turn. When the shoulders are completely turned back, allow the arms to begin falling, the wrists will relax and the club will fall to the three o'clock position (see fig. 5) just before the counterfall automatically occurs and the hip turn then whips the arms and club through impact. If you should happen to "whiff" the ball when you first attempt the drill, don't be surprised. You'll immediately feel how dependent you are on your arms to locate the ball. Without the proprioceptive input of the address, the arms feel

115

totally lost. Each time you hit another shot, back **completely** away from the ball (about six feet) and approach again. Once you get a feel for addressing the ball with your vision only, you will probably hit the ball more solidly from this drill than you do from your normal swing. Most of my students do. Practice until you can hit every club in the bag from this mode, swinging with as much clubhead speed as you wish. You should be able to hit the ball very hard from this drill.

To further isolate proper technique in your body, do this drill with either arm (pages 130-131) alone and/or in a multiple one-footed series if you can. To hit quality one-armed, one-footed, "no reference" shots, requires a near "perfect" swing. Keep after it! Your brain will figure it out by "feel."

An interesting phenomenon in almost everyone who uses upper body force in their swing, is that after first doing a "no reference" drill several times, upon returning to a normal swing mode they will hit the ball "fat." Through the drill, the brain seems to "erase" the underlinecompensating movements for back-pressure (energy turned into the body) that exists in their normal, arm-guided swing. Once the arms are trained out of the swing, one can go from a "no reference" mode to a normal mode and hit the ball perfectly.

Go out by yourself onto the golf course—or with someone else if you're not intimidated—and play out of a "no reference" mode on all of your full shots. You'll feel what a strong tendency we all have to "guide" the ball. Do this drill until you have the confidence to step up to the ball without an address, push that club up, turn your shoulders back and let it rip. This drill will teach you how to develop a super swing.

TRANSFER DRILLS

Transfer drills, when using both or either arm only on the club, are excellent for developing the 2:1 timing of the "Gravity" swing. As mentioned earlier, the weight transfers to the right leg and back to the left leg while the shoulders move only to the completion of the backswing. This timing provides the "coil" or "separation" which allows the lower body to power the delivery.

Transfer drills should be done with at least ten and preferably twenty-five or more balls lined up in a straight line (perpendicular to the flight line) about four inches apart. Begin the drill with the feet together, balls lined between the feet (see page 128, fig. 1). When you feel ready, extend and firm the arms, step to the right (about shoulder width) and as soon as the right foot is planted (not before), let the back and shoulders heave the club into motion. As the heave is begun, the left leg relaxes and at the point of first release, the left foot completely leaves the ground and the leg swings freely to the right. When the left foot almost touches the right foot, the leg immediately changes directions (the left foot neither hits the right foot nor does it touch the ground) and swings back to the left where the body lands on it exactly at the time when the shoulders reach full turn or separation (see fig. 6). When the left leg reaches the right leg and begins to change directions, it is important **NOT** to <u>step</u> back to the left, but to <u>fall</u> back. If the move left is made by stepping rather than falling, the weight will remain partially on the right side, preventing a complete loading of the left leg and reducing the starting momentum of the counterfall. Properly executed, the momentum of the body weight is deflected into the counterfall vector by landing onto and slightly against the left leg (as the shoulders complete their backturn), and the delivery and follow-through happen automatically.

When you reach the completion of the first swing, hold the finish position (see fig. 8) and watch the ball fly until it begins to fall (about three seconds). Remember, you **must** take time to breathe between swings. **Do not** re-address the next ball. From the finish position, step back to the right and enough forward (angled) to have the next ball in position, and as soon as the right foot is set, let the arms and club fall from the finish position and right into the backswing for the next shot. When the arms and club swing down and backwards past the next ball (don't accidentally hit it while making the backswing), the left leg breaks free from the ground and makes a full free flowing transfer just as it did in the first swing. Keep this rhythm going throughout the drill, remembering to breathe between shots. If you get out of sync, don't panic. Just relax and remember that there is plenty of time. The next ball will not sprout feet and walk away! If your grip moves out of kilter from a mis-hit, fix it while you're in the finish position and keep going from there. **Do not** re-address the next shot as you started in the beginning. Make yourself get into the next swing the way you got out of the last one. Not allowing yourself to re-organize and re-address each shot, forces the sub-conscious to take control of the drill and teach you the "treble-bass" timing (lower body moves over to the right and back, while the shoulders simply go back) of the

118

"Gravity" swing. Like in dancing the Cha-Cha, you don't want to be consciously thinking about what your feet are doing. Let it come by feel. You should continue swinging in the drill until all the balls have been hit.

One drawback of transfer drills is that in the two-handed mode, they can be faked. To be more specific, you can go through the weight transfer, then strike the ball with the arms and shoulders, instead of allowing the counterfall and pivot to clear the swing without effort. However, if you do the drill improperly, it is extremely fatiguing because the upper body labors around the heart. By putting enough balls in the line, you will quickly realize whether or not you are faking the drill, and will hopefully give up the tendency for violence. Don't give yourself a heart attack (which many people do annually — not my students — by swinging too violently) in an attempt to murder the ball. When you do this drill correctly, you'll be able to hit a high number of shots (above twenty) without discomfort or excessive fatigue. In truth, this drill could save your life by helping you develop an awareness of upper body force and violence in your swing. If you find yourself breathing heavily after just a few swings, you are using **too much** <u>applied</u> upper body action.

When you're fully trained, you should be able to control the ball (fades and draws) with every club using this drill, either in a two-armed mode or with either arm alone. The 2:1 timing of the transfer drills will quickly work it's way into the timing of your normal (feet spread and stationary) swing, without you needing to practice in that mode.

Learn the one-legged drills first to teach yourself basic swing fundamentals, then add the no reference and transfer drills to bring your swing up to it's full potential speed.

The various drills should be employed for at least **ninety percent** of your practice time until you are near being fully trained. **REMEMBER, THE EASIEST PRACTICE MODE TO FAKE OR TRAIN IMPROPERLY FROM, is a NORMAL SWING MODE (both hands on the club— both feet on the ground and spread). If you want to develop a great swing quickly — stay OUT of a normal swing mode and DO THE DRILLS.** Work on the drills that you do the **worst**. They are pointing out a weakness.

Don't forget that the drills are your "textbooks." They will tell you whether or not everything in your swing is compliant with the laws of physics, and show you how to fix it if there are problems. Study them carefully and they will teach you **everything** you need to know.

The author, David Lee, standing on the 14th fairway, overlooking the signature 15th hole of the beautiful Black Diamond Golf and Country Club, Lecanto, Florida.

Fig. 1

Fig. 2

Fig. 5

Fig. 6

Normal Swing. Adam Anthony

Fig. 3

Fig. 4

Fig. 7

Fig. 8

Fig. 1   Fig. 2

Fig. 5   Fig. 6

One footed, two handed drill.

Fig. 3

Fig. 4

Fig. 7

Fig. 8

Fig. 1   Fig. 2

Fig. 5   Fig. 6

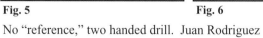

No "reference," two handed drill. Juan Rodriguez

Fig. 3

Fig. 4

Fig. 7

Fig. 8

Fig. 1

Fig. 2

Fig. 5

Fig. 6

Transfer drill.

Fig. 3

Fig. 4

Fig. 7

Fig. 8

Fig. 1

Fig. 2

Fig. 5

Fig. 6

Right handed, no "reference" drill.

Fig. 3

Fig. 4

Fig. 7

Fig. 8

131

Fig. 1

Fig. 2

Fig. 5

Fig. 6

Left handed, one-footed drill.

Fig. 3

Fig. 4

Fig. 7

Fig. 8

133

Fig. 1   Fig. 2

Fig. 5   Fig. 6

Right handed, one-footed wedge drill.

Fig. 3

Fig. 4

Fig. 7

Fig. 8

Fig. 1

Fig. 2

Fig. 3

Fig. 4

Right handed putting drill with wedge.

Chapter Seven

The Neurobiological Basis Of Gravity Golf

by Gregory A. Mihailoff, Ph.D.
Professor, Laboratory of Neurobiology
Departments of Anatomy and Neurology
University of Mississippi Medical Center

Authors Note: This chapter, although it is totally irrelevant to any golfer's ability to learn the GRAVITY golf swing, is quite fascinating in that it gives an insightful and highly educated viewpoint of why this teaching system is so effective. You may skip it altogether if you so desire, or, if you are interested in how your marvelous brain works, here's a qualified opinion.... with most of the medical and scientific language left out.... thanks doc!

Although most students of kinesiology or motor system control might agree that except for the most simple movements, willful or voluntary movement is probably initiated in the cerebral cortex, probably very few would agree on the precise *location* of the origin of movement. There is, however, a nearly limitless array of "voluntary" movements, some rapid, some slow, some complex, others relatively simple. Consequently, the mechanisms and brain locations involved in the regulation of this diversity of movement may also be quite variable. In athletics, with some exceptions of course, we might categorize movements that involve running or jumping as relatively simple compared to those that require some degree of eye and limb coordination. From a movement control perspective, hitting a baseball, shooting a basketball, or hitting a tennis ball or golf ball is equivalent in complexity to playing classical music on a piano or violin. Ironically, it is likely that each of these motor skills is *not* under the direct control of the motor cortex once the skill has been acquired or "learned." Of relevance then to our interest in the golf swing are three fundamental questions: 1) what brain systems are involved in acquiring and storing this complex motor behavior, 2) once learned, how is the skill improved and retained, and 3) what might be done to facilitate the learning and storage process. Unfortunately, the neurobiological information required to provide definitive answers to these questions is not yet available. What follows then is "reasonable speculation" based upon currently available information.

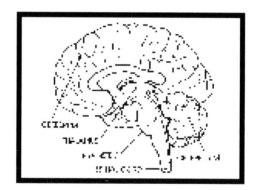

The areas of the brain that almost certainly play a major role in this process include the **spinal cord** and **brainstem**, the **cerebellum**, the **basal ganglia**, and motor areas of the **cerebral cortex** as well as related portions of the **thalamus**. In addition, the special senses of vision and equilibrium (balance) must also be important as well as cutaneous, proprioceptive (body position), and kinesthetic (body movement) sensory messages.

The precise neural mechanisms that underlie the "learning" or acquisition of any reasonably complex motor movement have not yet been described. Neuroscientists have shown that relatively simple muscle activity such as an eye blink can be learned quite readily. In a typical experiment, an animal can be conditioned or "trained" to make an eyeblink in response to a stimulus such as a tone or flash of light. There is some understanding of how the acquisition of this type of motor behavior takes place. However, an important question is whether this type of muscle activity should be considered as representative of voluntary motor activity. Rather, it seems reasonable that the learning of more typical kinds of voluntary movement involving numerous muscles acting across multiple joints must certainly utilize a more complicated neural substrate than eye blink.

WHAT IS THE NEUROLOGICAL BASIS OF GRAVITY GOLF?

In learning to make a typical multi-joint movement, two neurologically relevant points seem reasonably clear. First, the movement must be practiced and to be most effective, every repetition should be as true to the desired form as possible. Second, the "conscious" cerebral cortex control circuitry needs to be eliminated from the performance of the movements **as soon as is feasible**. So, is it possible to apply these two principles to the acquisition of the golf swing? In a word — **absolutely!** In fact, these same two principles form the basis of the GRAVITY swing and can be applied to the maintenance of proper swing mechanics and to our attempts to improve the golf swing after a set of fundamental swing conditions have been learned.

After working with David Lee for several years, it has become clear that **his teaching methods are perfectly suited to the development of the most biomechanically efficient swing parameters.** In short, the GRAVITY swing reduces the utilization of the conscious motor control system to the relatively simple task of initiating the backswing. A key element in the concept of GRAVITY GOLF is that the swing is learned and practiced from a *shrunken* safety envelope rather than from an expanded envelope, even though the latter might initially seem to be the more logical approach. *It is our belief that making it more difficult for the body to actually remain physically upright and stable, in essence forces the brain to direct and control the desired movement so that it is performed with as much biomechanical efficiency as possible, in order to prevent the individual from simply falling to the ground.* The vestibular system is responsible for maintaining balance and this function is largely performed in the background so to speak in cooperation with the cerebellum and without any conscious intervention. For example, while engaged in any common volitional motor activity such as walking across the street or going down a flight of stairs, an individual does not have to willfully think about maintaining the body in an upright posture. The nervous system accomplishes this task by superimposing the required muscle (motor) activity on a platform or posture that has been orchestrated by the vestibular system without any conscious effort from the individual. As the volitional movement becomes more complex and its performance makes it more difficult to maintain the appropriate balance or posture, then the vestibular system is forced to assume a more comprehensive role in directing the performance of the desired movement. It is surprisingly adept in this capacity, particularly if the individual is able to "relax" and inhibit the tendency to use the conscious control systems in an attempt to override the vestibular control mechanism. As balance and equilibrium are even more severely compromised, the conscious desire to override the vestibular system becomes stronger but paradoxically, the ability to consciously control the movement is more ineffective and the individual may actually fall to the ground or fail to perform the movement. We feel that this sequence of events in fact **explains why the GRAVITY GOLF teaching method is so successful.** For most individuals, standing on one leg and using one arm to maneuver the club as is required in the *Gravity Golf* drills is physically demanding to the point that in order to keep from falling to the ground, the individual must relax and avoid using the conscious control systems in order to allow the vestibular system (perhaps in concert with the cerebellum) to have essentially total responsibility for the movement. In this way the movement is performed with the **maximal degree of biomechanical efficiency.** The vestibular control mechanisms seem to have considerable influence over the larger, proximal muscles of the back and shoulders and the moment the individual makes a conscious effort to force the movement, usually by increasing the tension exerted by the hands and forearms, the result is a mis-hit or a fall off the pivotal axis. The individual should not "feel" that the hands and forearms are controlling the club movement but rather that they and the club are moving as a reaction to the centrifugal force created by the pivotal movement of the body. Slowly but steadily the swing is made with proper biomechanics that strictly adhere to the laws of physics, all the while being directed primarily by the vestibular system as it attempts to counteract the force of gravity and keep the individual upright.

Exactly how the vestibular system exerts this control over motor behavior is far from being understood, but a clue can be found in the fact that the vestibular system forms an extensive array of connections with the cerebellum. This portion of the brain is known to play an important role in the coordination of muscle function and it has also been implicated in the motor learning mechanism. In fact, because of its extensive connections with the cerebellum and other brainstem centers, it is likely that vestibular circuits are particularly well suited to the task of *altering* and *learning* a motor behavior. Although we often intuitively reason that the cerebral cortex must be in control of motor learning, it is becoming increasingly more evident that the cerebellum (both its cortex and deep nuclei) and related brainstem structures are important components in the formulation of certain types of motor memory but perhaps are not involved in the storage of motor memory. Thus in addition to **ensuring that proper mechanics are built into the golf swing** the GRAVITY method through its activation of the vestibular system and cerebellum, might utilize the most efficient and readily adaptive motor learning mechanism available in the central nervous system.

To what extent the so-called higher centers in the brain such as the motor-related areas of the cerebral cortex or the basal ganglia are involved in GRAVITY GOLF is less clear. To suggest that the GRAVITY swing must become totally "automatic" is perhaps an oversimplification. We might hope that certain of the "mechanical elements" of the swing would become essentially non-voluntary movements, but certainly on the golf course, a variety of sensory messages and thought processes must be integrated or linked with the motor program that actually directs the activation of the appropriate muscles. For example, grip pressure at address and the sense of relaxation or absence of tension in the arms at the "first release" are important components of the GRAVITY swing and are dependent upon conscious awareness of sensory signals from the skin and muscle sensors of the hands and arms. The conscious awareness or perception of these types of sensations occurs in the cerebral cortex and is dependent upon signals traveling along peripheral nerves and eventually up the spinal cord and brainstem. Other mental processes such as determining the distance the ball must travel as well as compensation for wind and the roll produced by the contour of the terrain must be incorporated into the "program" for each shot and these features are most probably directed by the cerebral cortex. Other problem solving situations that require for example, deciding whether to hit a draw or a fade, or a full seven-iron instead of a light six-iron are likely to require adjustments to the motor program that are directed by the prefrontal motor cortex based upon 1) sensory information it receives from other cortical areas and 2) its access to the memory of prior "motor" experience. This decision may involve connections that link the prefrontal cortex and the basal ganglia which then serve to alter the motor program. Finally, the act of starting the swing in motion is most likely initiated in the cerebral cortex.

The role of the basal ganglia in motor function is also very complex but recent experiments suggest that one of the primary functions of the basal ganglia is to **inhibit competing motor programs.** This is an interesting concept which means that in order for a movement to be performed, not only is it necessary for one component (certain muscles) to be activated, but other muscles must be deactivated or inhibited. Therefore, neural functions that involve an inhibitory mechanism have taken on added significance and such is the case with the basal ganglia. It now appears that one of the primary output signals from the basal ganglia is inhibitory at its termination site in the movement control centers of the thalamus, the neurons of which project to the motor cortex. Once thought to be involved in the initiation of involuntary movement, it now appears that at least one important function of the basal ganglia is to aid in the performance of motor activity by *inhibiting* those motor programs that would hinder or interfere with the desired movement. Inherent in this process is the possibility that the basal ganglia are also involved in some aspect of the motor learning (memory) circuitry.

SUMMARY

As an individual begins to develop and practice the GRAVITY GOLF SWING, a motor program that will control this movement is formulated within the central nervous system. Included in this program are the detailed plans for the activation of each of the muscles required to make this movement. The drills that comprise the GRAVITY training program aid the learning and performance of this complicated plan by introducing a maneuver (i.e. standing on one foot) which destabilizes the maintenance of upright body posture to such an extent that effectively, complete **control of the program passes to the vestibular system and cerebellum,** at least in terms of the basic mechanical elements of the swing. There are two principal advantages that accrue in this situation. First, it is known that the use of the conscious cortical control circuits is often ineffective in regulating rapid, complex movements, especially under stressful or fatiguing circumstances. By placing the body in danger of falling down, **we FORCE the brain to control the movement so that it is performed as efficiently as possible.** That means elimination of the cortical control system and the employment of **energy efficient biomechanics** in the swing parameters under the direction of the vestibular system and cerebellum. Perhaps because the vestibular system seems to have more direct access to the "motor learning" system as compared to the conscious control circuits, **not only is performance enhanced,** but also learning of the movement occurs **at a surprisingly rapid rate**. This is the second primary advantage of the GRAVITY system. Use of the drills during practice literally **forces the swing to become more "automatic" or consistent** since the vestibular system is in control of the movement under these conditions and this may **eliminate the errors introduced by our conscious attempts to tinker with or adjust components of the movement.**

Chapter Eight

The Finished Product
and
Playing Strategy

COMMUNICATION IS EVERYTHING

Neuroscience theories on how the brain teaches the body to acquiesce motor skills such as golf may be more than most players wish to know, but I personally find it fascinating that we are beginning to understand the complicated nuances of the human system.

The challenge for any technical instructor teaching motor movement, is to bypass as much of the verbal "jibberish" as possible and get the student to "feel" what the teacher is trying to communicate. This is not always easy (world's greatest understatement). Discussing the drills in chapter six, reminded me of an attempt at communication that ended with unexpected results.

In 1977 I had been working on the initial research of the Gravity teaching system for about two years and had been fortunate to receive the written endorsement of Jack Nicklaus on the concepts. As a result of that endorsement, Golf Digest had agreed to do a feature article on the system, if, I consented to do a clinic for their instructional staff. The clinic was to take place at Boca West in Florida where the Golf Digest team was conducting a golf school. The instructors at this particular school were Bob Toski, the late Davis Love, Jim Flick and Peter Kostis.

Although the clinic was scheduled for five o'clock, I had arrived early and was observing as the instructors were winding up the afternoon session. There were more than thirty people in the school, all of whom were gathered about Bob Toski and a not very physical lady of some sixty plus years. She was getting a little one-on-one lesson from him and the crowd was watching and listening as he taught her. Naturally, being the superb showman that he is, Bob was working to the audience—in fact—better than he was working her.

To say that this lady was limited in talent would be a kindness compared to what one might really be thinking. One thing she definitely was not limited in was jewelry. In my entire life I don't believe I've seen as many expensive baubles attached to one person. She had rings on every finger, necklaces, a broach, a watch that was covered in diamonds and fancy combs in her hair. Her gold earrings were the dangly kind, about three inches long and looked like they weighed about D-4. If she'd been able to generate any rotary speed on her follow through they could've slapped her up side the head and given her a concussion.

Rotary speed, however, was almost non-existent in her swing and at "full rip" with the driver she could hit the ball less than a hundred yards. She had no concept whatsoever of proper movement.

Toski watched her hit about five tee shots and could obviously see that any endeavor to overhaul her swing was going to take more effort and time than he was willing to invest. Alternatively, owning your own club manufacturing company (which he did and I believe still does) offers other

147

solutions to students who don't appear to be overburdened with talent, and he decided to seize the opportunity.

Having been extra quiet and attentive during her five swings, he suddenly reaches in his pocket and whips out a retractable steel tape measure. Bob measures her arms, her height, the distance from her fingertips to the ground, and then steps back to make a startling observation.

"You know what your problem is?" he asks. "No, that's why I'm here," she answers with a very serious deadpan look. Even though she already appears irritated, Bob is undaunted. "You're driving a dump truck," he says. "You're not built to drive a dump truck... you're built to drive a sports car... something you can handle! That'll take care of all your problems. What do you think about that?" he goes on. "How'd you like to be driving a sports car and feel some speed for a change?" She stares him down like a cobra and without even a hint of hesitation she sets him straight. "Mr. Toski, I've never driven anything but a Cadillac... and let me assure you... that's all I'm ever gonna' drive!" Bob can't open his mouth but turns to the crowd looking like Jack Benny with his chin resting on his hand and the whole place erupts in laughter. That was seventeen years ago and I still laugh when I remember the look on his face. Sorry Bob... no sale!

It doesn't take too many students like that little angel to make a golf instructor ponder his career choice, which is why I love teaching the Gravity Golf way. The drills do most of the tough communicating for me and I manage to maintain a white-knuckle grip on my sanity.

THE LOOK OF THE FINISHED SWING

As I mentioned earlier, the most fascinating thing about the drills is that they will totally train the finished mode (normal swing, pages 122-123) without practicing from conventional swing positions. Once proper swing sequencing has been trained into the "muscle memory" through the drills, you will find that when returning to the conventional mode (normal swing), correct movement will have developed **without** having practiced in that fashion. Proper technique seems to very mysteriously just "appear."

Characteristic of a properly functioning GRAVITY swing is not only a look of smoothness, but that of the center of mass remaining level both during the backswing and the follow through. The arms should go up in the backswing and down in the follow through without the body appearing to change levels. When this is done properly, the swing has a very <u>dynamic</u> looking flow where the change of direction between the backswing and delivery is hardly noticeable. The swing should never have an "upsy-downsy" look, but an appearance of level flow like that of an ice skater.

As a player's proficiency develops through practicing the various drills, an ability to execute shots either from a weight transfer mode or a non-transfer mode will also develop. The non-transfer mode (shots where **all** the body weight remains on the left leg throughout the swing) should be used on **all** shots of less than one hundred yards and may also be utilized on shots of even greater length with wonderful results, if, the player's technique is good enough to keep upper body force out of the swing.

Non-transfer shots around the green, and specialty shots, will be discussed in chapter nine.

ALIGNMENT AND BALL POSITION

During the course of explaining the swing in chapter five, I made little or no reference to ball position and alignment. In doing drills — especially one-footed drills — both problems have a unique way of taking care of themselves because of the rigid balance parameters.

Developing proper alignment and ball position are functions of first developing correct sequencing of movement between the body parts and then ingraining it to the point of consistency. Once your swing repeats from the same power source every time, the solutions to correct alignment and ball position become simple. To illustrate the point that alignment means very little without a consistent power source in the swing sequence, it should be noted that any number of golf balls can be hit from the same foot position and ball position, through about a ninety degree spread pattern, by simply altering the power source and degree of lateral movement from shot to shot.

This is certainly not an attempt to put anyone down — and you even see great players practice this way — but my first inclination when I see a player lay a club on the ground to check alignment, is a strong gut feeling that he/she doesn't know exactly how their swing works, or how it should work.

One can set his toes right against the club every time and still hit the golf balls all over the range. Once you develop proper sequence and a consistent power source — which the one footed drills teach — alignment and ball position have taken care of themselves. In clarification; when doing a one-footed drill, if the player lines him/herself up too far to the right of the intended target, there is a feeling of being "jammed" during the delivery and balance will be impossible to maintain. If, on the other hand, the alignment is too far left, one feels a need to "chase" the flightline with the club, and the **applied** motion to do so will cause balance loss and discomfort.

In the GRAVITY swing, the flightline of the shot is tangent to the arc of the swing, with the club moving on an inside, to square, to inside plane during delivery (fig. D, page 82).

If the ball position is placed too far back relative to the body's center of mass, the ball will go to the right of the target unless compensations are made. By the same token, if the ball position is too far forward relative to the body's center of mass, the shot will go to the left unless compensations are made. If both ball position and alignment are correct, the swing will feel "level" during the delivery, and assuming that the club face is square to the intended starting line at impact, the ball will release on that line.

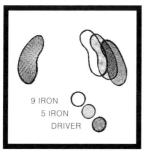

Fig. A Foot and Ball Positions

151

In going through a set of clubs from a driver to a wedge, the ball position will start approximately opposite the left heel for a driver and move slightly back and closer to the body for each successive club going down to the wedge (fig. A). Doing so accommodates plane changes in shorter clubs as well as greater time requirements in squaring the clubface on longer ones. As a general rule, the longer the club, the farther forward you need to play the ball.

SIDEHILL LIES

When taking your golf swing from the practice tee to the golf course, one of the first things you will encounter are all sorts of sidehill lies. It is not my intent to confuse anyone in regard to how players of varying power sources handle such situations — because it does vary — but suffice it to say that in the GRAVITY swing, we should treat all sidehill lies with greater left alignment and by moving the ball position back in the stance. Doing this allows us to remain on better "level" during delivery, by not "fighting" with the contour of the hill. Feeling and learning the subtle changes in alignment and ball position required to successfully negotiate various types of sidehill lies, can be easily accomplished through practicing one-footed drills off some of these different lies. You will immediately learn on a cognitive as well as a sub-conscious basis, how to accommodate the contour with your alignment and ball position. If you will practice various sidehill lies **from the drills** until you can hit the shots comfortably where you want, your alignment and ball position will be perfect. The proper feelings of alignment and ball position which you learn by doing one-footed drills from these lies, will automatically feed it's way into your two-footed, normal set-up.

152

PLAY FROM THE DRILLS

In fact, if your legs have enough strength, it is my strong recommendation — and something I do with my professional players — that you play one-footed until you become adept at it, **before** you consider trying to play on the course with both feet. You will become a good player **so much faster** that it will astound you. All the hazards, OB stakes and various other "goblins" we all worry about on the course, seem to disappear when you are on one leg. You'll immediately sense how much tension the course puts into you compared to the range, and the one-footed mode will teach you to deal with it. Your tendency to guide shots will disappear and you'll learn to trust your swing and "let go." If the one-footed drills are too strenuous, play from the no reference drill.

Once you become adept and comfortable at swinging the club from variable contours, "working" the ball left to right, or right to left will become relatively simple. When a GRAVITY player wants to hit a fade or a draw, it requires only slight changes in timing and alignment to do so.

FADES AND DRAWS

To fade the ball from the GRAVITY swing, the alignment should be slightly more open to accommodate the ball's movement toward the target. The grip does not need to change from normal, but in the swing itself, the heave intensity should slightly increase (to insure full rotation of the shoulders and an adequate counterfall), and the first release point (tension release) must be earlier. Doing so will cause the club to stall earlier and will slow the tumble rate of the club through the change of direction, allowing the wrists to cock slightly later than normal. This in turn enables the hip rotation to be slightly ahead of it's normal position through impact, causing the toe of the club to lag or be to some degree open when it meets the ball. Executed properly, the ball will track on the intended starting line until it reaches the apex of the arc, then fall gently to the right and toward the target. Ball position and timing determine the amount the ball will move, as well as the height of the shot.

A **properly** executed GRAVITY swing is essentially hook "proof" because there is no tension increase during the delivery to cause the plane reversal which would allow the toe of the club to pass the heel and produce a pull or hook. Assuming we **want** to draw the ball, which we often times need to do, it is again necessary to make slight alignment and timing changes. The body should be aligned whatever degree to the right of the target we wish to move the ball, with the stance slightly more closed to facilitate a "flatter," more inside plane on the takeaway. Heave the swing into motion as you would normally, but during the delivery, right at the point of the angular release of the club into impact, the pivotal torque from the left hip must stop. This causes the hands to "trip" and the toe of the club will gain on the heel coming into impact, producing a draw, or hook.

As mentioned throughout this book, the ability to hit controlled shots is enhanced by playing with passive hands. Hitting a draw creates activity in the hands and a "dead-heat" situation because of the rapid closing of the blade at impact. Develop a feel for doing this so that you're not limited in the types of shots you can play, **but don't "go to the well" too often.** Although draw shots will run farther on a hard fairway, they tend to get out of control more easily. A draw also has a tendency to bounce left significantly when it hits the green, whereas a fade lands softly.

Once a player has developed the ability to work the ball either direction at will, assuming there is some knowledge of the short game (next chapter), we are ready and capable of strategizing our way around the golf course. It was my original intent to discuss strategy in a separate chapter after the short game, but since this chapter is sort of short — and maybe you're tired of reading and want to run out for nine holes — let's do it now.

GOLF ARCHITECTS CAN BE NASTY

Golf architects **can** be the most wonderful individuals... building exciting, challenging and visually stimulating holes on which we can enjoy our sport. Or... some days they can wake up on the other side of the bed and decide to do something vile and devious! Sometimes Mother Nature herself can throw a few nasty natural nuances into a golf hole without the architect having to dream them up. When Alister MacKenzie built the sixteenth hole at Cypress Point, he didn't have to be too creative (taking nothing whatsoever away from him). All he really had to do was figure out how far you can carry a golf ball if you rip your insides out. The rest was simple! "Let's put a flat tee here.. a flat green over there on the other side of the Pacific.. a bail out area over there to the left for the pansies"... and that was about it! Actually, MacKenzie was pretty lenient. Pete Dye would have moved the green a few feet closer to the cliff and would have made it smaller.. and would have eliminated the bail out area. Jack Nicklaus would have moved the green farther out on the point to the right where only he and a few of his close friends could reach the green.. plus he'd have made the green three tiered so only he and Houdini could putt it!... Sorry... I'm doin' it again... getting carried away, that is...

The truth is, however, that architects do indeed add many little subtleties in the form of mounds, unseen water hazards, traps, and even key trees. Some of these features visually distort the true image of how the hole really lays out.

If you will discipline yourself to do what I am about to tell you, it will shave more strokes off your game than you might imagine.

How many times have you walked up to a green and found yourself plugged in a bunker face, twenty feet from the hole, staring double bogey right in the mouth... only to look at the green and realize that you had eighty feet or more on the other side of the hole from which you could have easily made par or maybe even birdie? Not only can we be "suckered" by difficult pin positions, the simplest areas of the green to hit can often times be obscured or distorted by traps or mounding, and we wind up attempting shots that not only stress our ability to the limit, they greatly diminish our odds of hitting the green..

CHART THE COURSE

Do this. Late some afternoon, when everyone is off the golf course, get a golf cart, two thin stakes at least three feet long with small flags on them, and a note pad. Drive to the landing area of the first hole, get out of the cart and look back at the tee. Then look at the landing area and study it for all it's features. Check the locations of any potential hazards — like traps, water, OB stakes, clumps of bushes or specific trees you wouldn't want to be near — and anything else which might cause a potential problem. Study the slope of the fairway and determine how the ball is going to react when it hits the ground. Look back at the tee again, studying the flight corridor of the shot, and figure the safest starting line for the shot if you aimed at that spot and the ball went there. Put a stake on that spot. It will generally be about five yards in the fairway on one side of the hole or the other. Now walk about twenty-five paces across the fairway and plant the other stake at a point beyond which you would not want the ball to roll laterally. When you play, assuming your ball starts at the first stake, lands and remains between there and the second stake, you should be fine. Most tee shots should be played to start on a safe starting line and move right to left or left to right. If you make a poor swing, your shot should stay on the starting line and may not curve the amount you intended — but it will be OK and in play. If it starts at the chosen line and moves the opposite direction from what you intended — go back to the practice tee! Using this strategy gives you

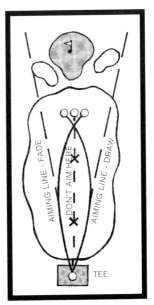

Fig. B Aiming Strategy

157

nearly the entire expanse of the fairway in which to work your shot and nearly double the margin for error than if you aim down the middle and try to hit it straight (see fig. B). A perfectly straight shot is one of the most difficult shots in golf to hit and very unpredictable from the standpoint of which direction it will go in the event of a mis-hit.

Now here's what's really interesting. After you've planted both stakes, get back in the cart, go back to the tee and look at the location of the stakes from there. Not always, but sometimes, the safe starting line (first stake) for the shot will be a considerable distance from where the visual deceptions of the hole may have led you to believe it was prior to setting the stakes. You need to establish a visual coordinate (something in the distance) on exactly where that optimum starting line is. If you don't think you'll remember, write it down on your course notes. On tee shots alone, knowing the perfect starting coordinant can save you one or more shots per round. If there are certain holes on your course which frequently give you trouble, you are probably being visually deceived into improper alignment and poor directional strategy by some aspect of the hole's architecture.

PLAY SMART

A few other notes on tee shot strategy: First, select a club for the tee shot that gives you the best odds of having a decent and simple approach into the green. It doesn't always have to be a driver. Secondly, when you have water on one side of the fairway and OB (out of bounds) stakes on the other, normally you should start the ball down the side with the water and work the ball toward the OB. The odds are greater that if you make a poor swing, your ball will go where you aim it, than they are that your shot will move from your starting line, across the fairway and OB on the opposite side. Hitting into a lateral water hazard is less penalizing (one stroke) than going OB (stroke and distance).

If you come to one of those friendly "development" golf holes with OB stakes on both sides of the fairway, pick your favorite way to work the ball, "gut up" and rip it! Your most aggressive, tension free swing is more likely to put it in the fairway than a frightened, tentative move.

O.K.... you know how to put your ball in play. Get back in your cart, pick up the two stakes in the fairway and drive to the green. Walk to the **back** of the green and study it from there looking **back toward the fairway.** Note the locations of key traps that you want to avoid, other hazards around the green, slopes which would adversely affect a shot, tilt angle of the green, ground firmness and grain direction of the grass. A shot landing into a slope and into the grain — especially if the green is soft, will spin back like crazy. All the opposites are true and the ball will land and take off. Consider as many affecting factors as you can think of, and then picture your shot flying from your chosen landing area in the fairway, to the green. Pick an exact spot, that all things considered, gives you the very best odds of staying out of trouble and getting down in no more than two putts if your ball were there, to any pin position on the green. Put one of the flagged stakes on that spot or get a friend to stand there.

Get back in your cart, drive back to the landing area where your tee shot is expected to be, and look at that stake or friend from there. On many different holes on the course, you will be **astounded** at how far that spot can be from where the architecture of the hole has led you to believe it is prior to staking it and having simply estimated the green's safest landing area from the fairway.

You need to have both a visual coordinant and a yardage to that spot on the green from a sprinkler head in the fairway near to where your tee shot should be.

The **smart** player, when he/she plays, will hit the club which will carry their ball to that point... **regardless** of the pin location.

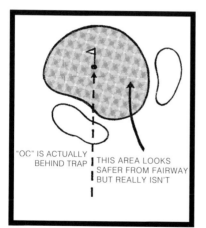

"OC" IS ACTUALLY BEHIND TRAP | THIS AREA LOOKS SAFER FROM FAIRWAY BUT REALLY ISN'T

Fig. C Optimum Green Centers

OPTIMUM GREEN CENTERS

My term for this spot on the green is the "optimum center." Players who can control the ball, should choose the club which will carry their ball to the "OC" and work the shot over it toward the hole. If the pin is to the right of the "OC," they will fade the shot. If it's to the left, they will draw it — but they will still work the ball **over** that point. If the pin is past the "OC," take the club which will carry the ball to the "OC" and clear the hip turn a little faster. The ball will go farther. If the pin is short of the "OC," still take the same club, but clear the turn more gently. Whatever you do, however, know **exactly where** that spot is, **how far** it is, and **USE IT** to strategize your shot. If you're in a tournament and can't get your breath, **forget the pin and hit the shot to the "OC."**

Some greens, because of size, have two optimum centers and you need to know where both of them are, with a yardage and visual coordinant to each.

Identifying optimum starting coordinants for your tee shots and optimum centers for each green, may seem like a lot of work, but you only need to do it once for each course where you're serious about shooting low scores. You'll be amazed how much better your numbers will look on the scoreboard if you take this seemingly boring, faint hearted approach to playing. Most professional players, with **large** bank accounts, do this in one form or another. As you know your swing better, you'll learn **when** to be aggressive, **when** to be conservative, **and the extent of your limitations and capabilities.**

GET IN, GET OUT

One of the **most important** things good players learn, is that when they occasionally do get into trouble, to be absolutely certain that on their next shot they play conservatively enough to get **completely out** of trouble. If you try to be a hero too often by attempting a near impossible shot to save par, you'll find double and triple bogies on your card. The smart player accepts bogey when it is staring him in the face and avoids the big number. Making a five on a par four hole is a lot more palatable than a seven or eight after your second shot ricochets off a tree out of bounds, because you tried to hit a three foot gap between two trees thirty yards in front of you in an effort to make a heroic par! I'll admit that it does make your chest swell a bit when you pull one of those shots off, but the player who doesn't believe he/she can get "up and down" from a hundred and twenty-five yards after a chip-out, should have a "back-up" profession.

WATCH OUT FOR THIS

Before we leave this chapter, there is one other noteworthy negative effect that course architecture and natural terrain can have on the swing. Holes where the fairway or green are elevated, tend to cause the player to swing "up" at the ball to accommodate the change in elevation. If you get your swing out of "level" through the impact area, you'll increase the tendency to pull or block the shot. Any time the fairway or green lies above you, line up slightly more left, move the ball position back in your stance a little and open the blade of the club slightly at address. Keep your swing in sequence and "level." The opening of the blade will add enough additional loft to the ball trajectory to allow for the elevation increase in the terrain, and the "level" swing will track the ball right at the intended target line.

Now... in the unlikely event that with all this good stuff in our heads we might still miss a green now and then, it would behoove us to know how to play some of those fun little short shots to get the ball onto the putting surface. Oops... did I say putting? Oh my yes... that exasperating part of the game where subtlety is enormous, technique incredibly varied, and the laws of physics crucified. Shall we talk about some of that brain-twisting stuff? Next page please...

Chapter Nine

The Short Game
and
Putting

COME AGAIN?

A long time ago I decided that when I wrote this book it would include the story of Mr. Ng (sounds like ung without the u). This seems about as good a place for it as any.

My long time friend, Greg Powers, who's been trying to reach his potential (which was tremendous until he shattered his left hip socket in an auto accident in 1992) on the tour for about twenty years or so, tells this story about a pro-am in Singapore. It may not translate that well to the page, but anyone who has ever heard it will attest that everyone in the vicinity of Greg when he tells it, needs oxygen to keep from dying laughing.

Greg's one of those people who is always late—everywhere he goes—and drives like there is no tomorrow to get there. Some years ago he was playing in a pro-am on the Asian tour and sure enough, was about to miss his starting time. He and his caddy make it to the first tee just as they are about to call an alternate to take his place. Naturally, Greg is already wound up and excited. When he gets that way he talks about a mile-a-minute and his voice can be pretty loud and abrupt. As he scurries to the check-in table, he's intercepted by the starter. The starter introduces himself and Greg quickly responds "how-do-you-do-I'm-Greg-Powers." He then proceeds to introduce Greg to his three amateur playing partners. "Mr. Powers, this is Mr. So-and-so." "How-do-you-do-I'm-Greg-Powers." The starter goes to the next guy. Mr. Powers, this is Mr. So-and-so." Greg is ready to be done with the intros so he can swat it and responds even quicker. "Howdy-Greg-Powers." Finally, the starter turns to the third fellow who is a very quiet and shy looking Oriental gentleman and says.. "Mr Powers, this is your other playing partner, Mr. Ng." Greg hurriedly reaches out his hand and then stops dead in his tracks. He looks right at this guy, hesistates for about three seconds and says...... "WHAT?..... what did he say your name was?" The man kind-of bows politely and says.. "my name is Ng." Greg just stands there stupefied and asks again..... "Did you say.... Ng?" Mr. Ng responds once more.. "yes... Ng." By this time Greg's forgotten all about teeing off. He gets right in the man's face. "What kind of a name is.... Ng?" Still politely, Mr. Ng replies.. "it's just my name... Ng." Greg stays right on him. "How do you spell Ng?" Calmly, Mr. Ng answers him again. "Just like it sounds... N... g." Greg's getting flustered now and starts talking fast again. "That's-not -even-a-word... it-doesn't-have-any-vowels! I can't say it very loud.... Ng..... Nnng..... NNNNG!" Greg's really on him now. "We're not gonna' be able to play together!" Mr. Ng quietly asks.. "why not?" "Cause you're gonna' be on one side of the fairway and I'm gonna' be on the other.... we won't know who's away.... and I'm gonna' yell... hey NNNG!..... are you away NNNNG!..... or am I away..... NNNNNG!? You won't be able to hear me! I'll be yellin' at the top of my lungs! Oh... NNNNNNG!!! You'll just be standin' there! We'll never finish!" Greg has these huge eyes that sort-of bug out when he gets excited and by now he has everyone on the tee laughing so hard that tears are running down their faces.

Suddenly, a very quiet, nice looking lady appears and walks over to Greg and Mr. Ng. "How do you do," she says in a whisper. "Is there a problem? My name is Mrs. Ng." Greg's eyes bug out about an inch farther! "OH ... NOOO! .... another one .... TWO NGS!" Greg throws up his hands, walks over to the tee and promptly tops his drive about eighty yards down the fairway. Watching it dribble away he mutters.... "oh NNNG!"

PITCHES AND CHIPS

The technique Greg used to hit that eighty yard miscue, is not exactly what I've got in mind for shots of that distance. Unfortunately, a great many golfers would feel just about as comfortable standing over an eighty yard pitch with a driver, as they do with a sand or pitching wedge.

The reason that so many players have an abiding fear of these delicate shots is because they utilize improper physics when attempting to execute them. Couple that with how close to the hole we're expected to hit the ball compared to an acceptable result for a tee shot (most anywhere in a thirty yard fairway — exact distance not critical) and zap... we're terrified! The slightest swing-plane movement can cause a fifty yard pitch — which we are trying to hit within five or six feet of the hole — to miss the green altogether and perhaps plug in a greenside bunker or fall short into a pond. How embarrassing! How humiliating! Little wonder tension creepeth in.

Here's where the mechanical problems usually lie. As I mentioned in chapter five, we've been historically taught that the key to short shots is to stand **still** over them.

HOGWASH! Not to be redundant, but this is worth further discussion because of the demanding physics parameters required to **consistently** execute delicate shots. What we want is a **NET APPEARANCE of stillness in the body,** created by proper counterfall and the resulting equilibrium in the pivotal axis during delivery. Remember that the **key** word in the third law of motion, which says, **for EVERY action, there is an equal and opposite reaction,** is **EVERY**. The **ARMS MUST MOVE** to hit any shot, and the pull against the body by the arms and club during the delivery requires a counterfall to offset those forces and maintain an "appearance" of stillness. Doing this properly enables us to keep the club perfectly in plane and to contact the ball exactly in the "sweet spot" of the clubface.

Review the paragraphs on counterfall in chapter five, and remember that unless there is a proper counterfall, the delivery cannot be accelerated without a muscle flex, which throws the club out of the swing-plane.

Remember also that no normal shots inside of eighty to one hundred yards require a weight transfer to easily reach the target. As in a one-legged drill, the counterfall from the left leg only, combined with the fall of **tension free** arms and the power of angular wrist release, allow enough power to be generated by the forward pivot to cover the distance **without** effort. A weight shift on these shots can provide so much momentum that it becomes necessary to throttle the club acceleration with arm and wrist tension and doing so causes swing-plane movement.

Varying the distance for short shots should be controlled by **decreasing the duration** of the heave, **not** by decreasing its intensity to hit it shorter. Most players are tentative starting the backswing for short shots and subsequently do not get **all** the tension out of their arms and wrists (big trouble). Even on **very** short shots, we need an abrupt or powerful heave to start the shoulder rotation which carries the body into the counterfall, as well as the certainty that there is **NO LIFT from the hands** resulting in tension when the arms are ready to start down (the arms won't fall if there is). The heave can be powerful, but if the duration is short, the arms won't go back too far for the length of the shot.

Remember that arm tension in the downswing creates leverage resistance to pivotal motion in the downswing and subsequent swing-plane movement. If arm tension in the delivery causes the pivotal rotation of the body to momentarily stop, only the weight of the arms and club hit the ball (a fraction of the body weight that is available), and the shot may come up short. Assuming set-up and posture are proper, if the heave intensity and duration are correct, the proper amount of arm travel in the backswing will occur, the wrists cock automatically when the first release occurs, and the counterfall begins the delivery **without** effort. Maximum available body weight is released into the shot and both accuracy and distance will be precise.

In all short shots where no weight transfer and reduced backswing arm travel are employed, the right elbow does **not** fully release and re-route as in a full swing (weight transfer), but remains in a down or "connected" position throughout the takeaway and delivery. In a full swing there is time for the right arm to drop back into a "connected" position while the body's weight shifts from the right leg back to the left leg. In a short shot, we don't need the extra arc leverage provided by a full right arm release, nor the late wrist cock that accompanies it. Timing becomes too critical if the right arm gets excessively far from the body in a short shot, plus the added power can cause us to decelerate the swing with arm and wrist tension if we sense that the shot is going to go too far—then all sorts of problems can occur (starting with swing-plane movement).

Pitch shots, or shots where we want to carry and land the ball softly, generally should be played from an open stance position, with the weight totally on the left leg. The weight should be on the **hip** muscles, **NOT** the quadriceps above the knee. Proper pivotal rotation will not occur during the delivery if the quadriceps are too heavily loaded and the weight is on the ball of the left foot instead of the **heel**. The right leg serves only as an anchor to the forward pivot, to keep the follow-through momentum from carrying us off the left leg.

The hands should be in a slight forward press position to allow for an earlier wrist cock in the swing. The shorter the shot, the less arm travel we need in the takeaway, the quicker the wrists must be cocked by the heave momentum, and the more forward press we need.

From a standpoint of ball action, the major difference between a chip shot (sometimes called a "bump and run"), is in the amount of backspin on the shot after it lands. Pitches stop quickly, chips release and roll. To hit a soft pitch with a wedge or any other lofted club, the shoulder heave at the start of the backswing, should receive enough help from the hands, to throw the toe of the club open as it goes back. This results in a softer, more glancing blow to the ball at impact, producing backspin.

Chip shots are generally played with the ball farther back in the stance (de-lofting the club), and the swing-plane is slightly more to the inside. The toe of the club is not thrown open and the shot is struck with a more direct blow. When the ball lands, it will "release" and "run."

Pitch shots are generally played to stop as quickly as possible after the ball lands. The general rule on chips is to select the club that will safely carry the ball over the fringe of the green (about three feet), and still have it stop rolling by the time it gets to the hole (fig. A). Hitting the green with a shallower angle of decent

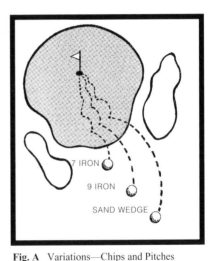

Fig. A Variations—Chips and Pitches

usually gives a better feel for distance and leaves less factors to chance (soft spots, etc.).

BUNKER AND SPECIALTY SHOTS

Bunker shots (sand) and pitch shots out of heavy rough around the green, are unique in that the ball does not compress to the degree that it does in other shots where the back of the ball is struck cleanly by the club. Therefore, both types of shot require a little "insurance." In the follow-through, the body should turn a full ninety degrees (facing target) on all these shots, even very short ones. The full body turn through, "excavates" the area around the ball and will advance the shot with minimum aid from ball compression. The arms should **NOT** tighten and create the risk of reducing body rotation or the ball may come up short of the hole (or be blasted long by a moving swing-plane and clubhead).

All short shots, including bunker and rough shots, should be learned and practiced from the one-footed drills as described in chapter six. By doing so, you will develop an incredibly deft touch around the greens, the ability to cope with any lie, and you'll shave bunches of strokes off your scores.

Initially, short shots are much easier to play from one leg than they are from two. This is because once the right leg is set on the ground, it creates rotational resistance both back and through, which you will have to learn to overcome through a more aggressive heave. These shots can be practiced with either or both arms on the club from the one-footed mode (pages 134-135). After you become adept at one-footers, you may practice in a two-footed, either arm mode. When you practice right handers in the short game, start the club from it's normal position behind the ball (page 134, fig. 1) instead of the three o'clock position of the full swing right handers (we don't want the elbow to leave the down facing position and get too far from the body).

My strong recommendation is that while your learning this, hit all your short shots on the course from the two-handed, one-footed mode. You'll be amazed at how much better your results will be than if you have both feet on the ground. When you're technically ready to go into a two-footed, normal mode, you'll know it. If you are still "chilly-dipping" or "blading" any of these shots when you go to the normal mode, go back to using the drills until your technique improves.

PUTTING

Why is putting so darned confusing to people? For this reason! There are a lot of technically poor putting methods that will knock the ball into the hole if the physics errors are compensated. It is very difficult to watch someone putt a golf ball and ascertain the quality of their physics, because of the subtlety of movement. Obviously, one can putt successfully many different ways, but the truth is, the better the physics employed, the better the stroke will hold up under pressure, year in and year out.

We're told constantly by "experts" on TV that gifted putters like Raymond Floyd and Ben Crenshaw are born, and that their level of skill cannot be duplicated or learned by the average player. **Double hogwash! TRIPLE HOGWASH!** Almost anyone can learn to putt as well as those two gentlemen, **IF**... they know **EXACTLY WHAT** to practice, and **HOW** to practice it! The only reason most players can't putt the way Ben and Raymond do, is that golf technology heretofore has not been able to explain the enormous subtleties of **what they are doing differently** that enables the increase in deftness of touch.

Players hammer on me all the time. "Look at that guy! According to you, David, his mechanics are awful... but watch how well he putts." My reply is... yes... he does putt well. But... if he had technically compliant physics and had **NO** energy turning back into his body during the stroke to throw the swing-plane off and create deceleration, how good **COULD** he putt? The most difficult thing for any instructor to do is to convince someone who is successful at any aspect of the game, that they **could be better with BETTER TECHNIQUE**. Young pros glare at me. "I hear what you're sayin,' but are you gonna' _____ up my putting stroke," they ask? No, I come back. It's already _____ed up (put any words that suit your taste in those blanks.. my preference is mess), but you're plodding blindly along in the dark of mechanical ignorance and don't know it! Are you making any money... I ask? "No... but I'm close." Logic aboundeth! Just relax I tell them... if it ain't broke, I won't fix it! What they usually want is **not** mechanical understanding but a little pixie dust!

Regardless of what D.P. says (those initials don't stand for Doris Popachek), **if you are** swinging the putter back on the flightline and through on the flightline, you are in CONFLICT with proper physics. All that straight back and straight through brainwashing, and the expensive little devises that help you do it, might make you putt better, but they **won't** make you putt **as well as you can**. Remember that unless gravity (counterfall) and rotational torque from within the pivotal axis (left leg) provide the power, the stroke **cannot** be made with maximum energy **efficiency**. If you get your power and touch from the same place (hands, arms and shoulders) by pushing the putt down the line, you will decrease your touch. When the power comes from within the axis, the hands remain free to do nothing but feel.

Just as in other shots, the proper swing-plane arc should be slightly to the inside on the takeaway, back to square at impact, and inside on the follow-through, with the ball releasing on a tangent line to that arc.

Posture in the GRAVITY putting stroke (page 174) should be fairly erect with all the weight on the left leg just as in pitch and chip shots. The stance should be slightly open with the left foot turned about thirty degrees to the left to facilitate the forward rotation, and the left knee slightly flexed.

Just like the other shots, the heave sets the swing into motion and the **duration** (not the intensity alone) of the heave determines the distance of arm travel and thus ball travel (green speed is also a factor). There should be absolutely NO tension increase in the arms or wrists during the delivery and the power comes **strictly** from the counterfall (gravity) and pivot (centrifugal force). On a putt, the pivotal movement will be so subtle that unless you're really looking closely you won't even see it. There will be **no** flexing forces to throw the swing-plane out of track and the ball off line.

If you've ever noticed that when some players hit a putt, it seems to keep rolling easily after you would expect it to stop, you've witnessed a characteristic of the GRAVITY putting stroke. In this stroke, all the available body mass goes into the shot, compared to only the weight of the hands, arms and putter in a typical stroke where you stand still and push it down the line. The golf ball is an object at rest when it is sitting

Fig. 1

Fig. 2

Fig.3

Fig. 4

Gravity putting stroke.

on the green and has resistance to being set into motion. The more body mass you release into the shot, the greater will be the predictability of distance, and the less effort will be required to cover that distance.

There is one other notable difference between a putting stroke and a golf shot which we should discuss. In a golf shot, because of the greater distance we stand from the ball, the left hand and forearm are able to supinate (rotate left - palm turning up) while the right hand and forearm pronate (rotate left - palm turning down). Together, the wrists release. The left hand actually rolls out of the way of the right wrist release.

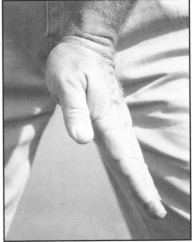

Photo B

In a putt, however, the plane of the swing is so steep because the ball is close to the body, that the left hand **cannot** roll out of the way of the right wrist release and actually begins to "jam" at about the point of impact (see photo B). This can cause an **unintended** deceleration of the club through impact and cause the putt to come up short as well as the line being thrown off.

By practicing right arm only putting drills, you can easily see that during the stroke, the right wrist releases better without the left hand being on the club. However, when one gets nervous under pressure, it is difficult to putt one-handed.

What we need is the ability to place the left arm on the club for the swing-plane stability of triangulation, **without inhibiting** the release of the right wrist in the stroke. This can be accomplished by gripping the club with a much softer grip in the left hand than in the right hand, and being certain that **no tension** gets into the left wrist or hand either during the heave or the forward stroke. Only the right wrist is firm in the heave, and it too releases it's tension at the first release point. Gravity and centrifugal force **only** should power the stroke with **NO** wrist tension. The wrists should be tension free on **ALL** length putts. Vary the distance **not** by throttling the delivery with tension, but by hitting the first release sooner after the heave (to hit it shorter).

THE "YIPS"

Since I don't wish to end this chapter on this subject, I'll save the putting drills for last. I'd just as soon discuss hemorrhoids or carrot and raisin salad as talk about the "yips," and those of you who have never had them can just ignore this part — **but don't forget where it is!**

The "yips" are not caused by bad nerves as is commonly believed and they can occur on any short shot. **They are the result of improper mechanics.** That is not to say that they won't make you nervous or apprehensive... to the contrary. In fact, they have ruined the enjoyment of golf for many people as well as the careers of many prominent playing professionals.

Here's what happens. The problem begins when the takeaway is made with the hands and arms instead of the back and shoulders. By not originating the takeaway, the shoulders and back will usually be too relaxed when the takeaway begins. When the back muscles are stretched by the arms going back, being elastic, they (back muscles) will naturally rebound slightly when the top of the backswing is reached. When the back muscles rebound, they cause the clubhead to rebound about an inch or so also. When this happens, the **true** top of the backswing is the position of the shoulders, arms and clubhead **after** the rebound has occured. Not having anticipated this rebound of the club, the brain senses that the delivery is leverage deficient. In other words, the backswing is now **too short** for the club to come up to adequate speed by the time it reaches the ball, for the shot to reach the target. Sensing this leverage deficiency coming into impact, the subconscious causes the hands to physically grab or flinch (tighten) in order to make up the leverage loss, and the results are disastrous! The ball will either explode off the clubface and go too far, or the swing-plane reversal may cause the player to hit behind the shot — possibly even double hit the ball.

In any event, this is a truly horrible feeling and this is the voice of experience speaking. Playing in the Texas Open at Pecan Valley C.C. in San Antonio in 1971, on the fifth hole, I stepped up to a dead flat putt of no more than five feet... and "yipped" it fifteen feet past the hole! My next swing tossed the putter softly toward my caddie. It was the only time in my life that I ever walked off the golf course. The good news is... that I discovered what caused the "yips," and when I learned how to handle my short clubs and putter **correctly**, the dreaded "disease" left me completely. Today I'd match my short game with just about anyone. Learning to use the GRAVITY swing and putting stroke will eliminate the "yips" because the poor mechanics which cause them do not occur. Let's move to a more pleasant topic — like what drills will teach you to putt like a tournament winner.

PUTTING DRILLS

The flat face of a putter tends to mask technical errors in the stroke and the subtlety of detecting swing-plane movement (which will make putts miss) or deceleration is enormous.

To magnify your errors so that your stroke can become technically "perfect," do this. Take your sand wedge and your putter, and a bunch of golf balls, to the lowest part of your practice putting green. Take your sand wedge first, posture yourself as described in the section on putting techniques, and begin putting with the right arm only (page 136). Putt the balls as far as you can (at a hole), uphill across the green, contacting the ball **exactly** on it's equatorial axis with the blade (leading edge) of the wedge. This is **extremely** difficult to do if your technical mechanics are not perfect — and would be next to impossible to demonstrate consistency. If the ball jumps up in the air, or if you top it, either the ball position and alignment are off, or you are sending energy back into your body by tightening the arm or wrist during the delivery. Practice with the wedge and the right arm only, until you can consistently putt a dozen balls into a circle no larger than three feet in diameter, from at least sixty feet. When you make a perfect stroke, the ball will roll off the blade of the wedge **just as well** as it does off a putter.

Remember to begin the drill from a long distance going uphill. Short and downhill putts can be technically faked. Once you learn to putt properly from a distance with the wedge, and then move closer to the hole, you'll know if you are faking it. Don't worry about practicing this drill wrong. If you use improper mechanics, you won't get the ball anywhere near the hole. Experiment until you get results. When you do, you will be using proper technique.

After you become adept at putting right-handed with the wedge, add the left hand to the club and putt (still from a distance) with both hands. You will feel how the left hand and wrist tend to inhibit the right wrist release and cause deceleration of the clubhead. Learn to keep your left from interfering when it goes onto the club.

Once you become a putting demon using the blade of the wedge, go through the same procedure with your putter. Start in a right-handed mode (still from a distance) and move into a two-handed normal mode only after you become deadly in the three other drills.

The drills are the key to isolating technically correct mechanics in your putting, short game and full golf swing. They will tell you amazing things about your body and how to control your movements... Allow them to teach you.

By the way... **great putters are made**... not born.

When all is said

When the cute stories are all told and the questions of how the parts should work have been answered with the best of my or anyone else's knowledge, there nevertheless remains the stark reality of getting yourself out to the driving range and the short game area, and making it all come together. All the money in the world and all the answers to the long-standing riddles, **will not** exempt you, me, Jack Nicklaus or anyone else from the disciplinary task of training the muscle memory to the point where the swing will hold up under great pressure. Some players are fortunate enough to "stumble" across the avenue to a physics correct swing without the technical understanding of exactly how it works, and still are able to harness it to the point of enjoying gratifying and prosperous careers.

Greater athletic skill and superior hand-eye coordination can play a major role toward enabling these gifted individuals to excel beyond what most of us achieve. Nobody ever said life was fair! Nevertheless, they have still paid their dues to the practice tee. Many more players come to within mere inches of seeing their golf goals and lifelong dreams solidify into reality, only to reel in horror and disappointment as the various cups pass to other hands before their outstretched fingers. Because of the most minute and subtle failures in understanding and discipline, thousands of careers that almost make it to a level we classify as "successful" or "outstanding," fall a little short.

My heartfelt belief is that there are many, almost great players, who might well have the personal drive to reach their dreams, **if** they were armed with a better understanding of how the swing **should** work and **how** to train themselves.

For me personally, when I discovered the existence of the first release and the counterfall, **all** of the mysterious pieces of the puzzle began to fall into place. Soon afterwards, the cloud of confusion which had hung over me for years, lifted, and the entire picture of how the "machinery" is supposed to work became crystal clear. Even today, I hit squirrely shots now and then — sometimes frequently — but now when it happens I know exactly why. And what's of greater importance, the more I practice **properly**, the better my execution becomes. Unfortunately, age is about to catch me! Well... what the heck... nobody escapes.

Whether your goal is to become a great player, or just to break ninety, the answers and secrets to mechanical perfection, in total compliance with the physical laws, are in this book. Even if you've read it once and don't believe it, trust me, they're in here. Read it again if necessary, and again and again, until it makes perfect sense. Granted, the human body is a **very** complex machine — but a machine nonetheless — with definitive answers to how it works. If you read it ten times and it still seems complex... DO THE DRILLS, and your wonderful brain will teach you perfectly... in spite of the complexity!

There's a lifetime of study contained within this offering. It represents a range of mental and physical states that began with groping and frustration, witnessed years of painstaking discovery, and culminated with the satisfaction of finally getting it on paper and into print. Believe me, I don't claim to know it all. Every day teaches me something new, with better ways to communicate to others. However, I can honestly say that I'm finally at peace with golf... and somewhat at peace with this book. It is my legacy to my profession, a love gift to the game I cherish, and my personal offering to you.

Take the knowledge, head for that beautiful green laboratory, and enjoy.

Notes